The Fine Art

RIO GRANDE VALLEY
LIBRARY SYSTEM

D1441685

The Fine Art of Découpage

LYN COCHRANE

SALLY MILNER PUBLISHING

RIO GRANDE VALLEY
LIBRARY SYSTEM W

DEDICATION

For Ruby and Dot,
my grandmother and mother
who fostered in me a love
for creating things of beauty.

First published in 2001 by
Sally Milner Publishing Pty Ltd
PO Box 2104
Bowral NSW 2576
AUSTRALIA

© Lyn Cochrane 2001

Design by Anna Warren, Warren Ventures Pty Ltd, Sydney
Edited by Anne Savage
Photography by David Young

Printed in Hong Kong

National Library of Australia Cataloguing-in-Publication data:

   Cochrane, Lyn (Lynette), 1944- .
   The fine art of decoupage.

   Bibliography.
   ISBN 1 86351 259 4.

   1. Decoupage. I. Title. (Series : Milner craft series).

745.546

All rights reserved. No part of this publication may be reproduced, stored in a
retrieval system, or transmitted in any form or by any means, electronic,
mechanical, photocopying, recording or otherwise, without prior permission of
the copyright owners and publishers.

Disclaimer
The information in this instruction book is presented in good faith. However, no
warranty is given, nor results guaranteed, nor is freedom from any patent to be
inferred. Since we have no control over the use of information contained in this
book, the publisher and the author disclaim liability for untoward results.

Acknowledgements

I wish to acknowledge the support given to me by my family and friends, especially to my creative découpage friends who are an ongoing source of inspiration:

- Members of the Découpage Guild, Queensland, especially Myra Givans and Alan Press who encouraged me and read my work.

- Melbourne découpeurs and friends, Joan McKenzie and Val Lade, whose expertise is always generously and graciously shared.

- Nerida Singleton, who taught me and many others the fine points of découpage and originally suggested I write this book. Access to her library was invaluable.

- Thanks to my sister Beverly, who read the draft and encouraged me to persevere.

- Special thanks to my daughter Maree. Her constructive criticism and admiration for my work has been the catalyst which has enabled me to constantly strive and take creative risks.

- Most especially, I wish to thank my husband John who has constantly ensured that my writing survives any computer hazards and has acted as secretary throughout the writing process.

Contents

Preface

From the earliest times decoration has been an integral part of design. Craftspeople as diverse as Chinese potters, prehistoric weapon-makers, mediaeval and eighteenth century furniture makers have always incorporated decoration in their designs. Decorations were very often functional as well, decorative handles for example, and were made using simple geometrical patterns, figures of men and animals and other basic shapes. They distinguished objects, showed ownership and in the case of weapons were often meant to magically attract the animal which the weapon was made to kill. Hand-made objects produced with great skill and patience have always been valued. The master designers of the past understood every technique of their craft and were trained over a very long period of time.

Through the ages decoration has often denoted wealth and power. Ornate buildings, especially homes, garments and jewellery could indicate great wealth. Decorated objects such as medals were used to honour those who had achieved at the highest level. Religion in particular provided great scope for decoration. The adornment of churches, sacred objects and statues, and the ornate depiction of religious stories and myths, reflected the great wealth within the Church and the importance of religion in people's lives. Toward the end of the Middle Ages art became more secular in character and decoration took on greater political and patriotic significance.

Understanding the techniques and acquiring the skills through much practice were the prerequisites to becoming fully qualified and respected craftspeople, who became one with their tools. Using their acquired skills, many craftspeople developed spontaneous and innovative designs which produced amazing results. But sadly, in time, the cost of hand-made objects became prohibitive and buyers began to favour mass-produced and cheaper goods. Too many skillful craftspeople found themselves on the outer because only the wealthy could afford the luxuries they produced, often purchasing them for reasons other than their beauty—their motives including the ostentatious display of power and wealth.

Modern designers can only marvel at the craftsmanship displayed in the work of the early designer–craftspeople. To produce such works of art today, when time has become the master of the product, seems almost unreasonable and improbable. Those who choose to be faithful to the original techniques of the hands, however, know the rewards—their creative spirits are nurtured and their hours of devoted work result in designs truly unique, objects of great beauty. Découpage is one of those techniques of old, in which the painstaking hours of work required result in the most beautiful and satisfying results.

There is no such thing as 'quick' découpage. Time must be spent locating both a well-designed object to work on and the motifs or images to suit it. The motifs must be cut, a unified design worked out and, once the motifs are glued in place, a series of layers of varnish applied and sanded until all the elements become as one, with a marble-smooth finish.

There are many ways to create découpage. Specialised techniques include elevation (or *vue d'optique*) which gives a three-dimensional effect achieved by layering one cut image over another to build up the level. Another technique called repoussé or moulage involves moulding and indenting an image from behind to give a raised or sculptured effect.

Around the world, beautiful découpage is being created still, sometimes in the most unlooked-for places. Tutors and workshop leaders who have mastered special techniques or

A large glass platter with découpage under glass and featuring a sponged painted background (see page 67).

who have expertise in a particular area such as colour, painting, or a knowledge of art, will provide that extra help which will encourage découpeurs and promote découpage so it will survive into the next century.

The découpage featured in this book is all my own work. Whether under varnish or under glass, the pieces all feature the special painted backgrounds which are my main subject. I have worked my découpage and background finishes on all kinds of surfaces—including timber, plastic, ceramic, plaster, glass, metal, plasterboard and craftwood.

We can learn from each other as we overcome difficulties to achieve our aims. The ideas in this book are culled from my own experience and that of fellow découpeurs and will, I hope, be of assistance to both the experienced and those attempting découpage for the first time.

INTRODUCTION:
The history of découpage

Découpage has a long history, with numerous examples dating back to early China, Persia and Italy. The production of découpage reached its highest point in eighteenth century Italy, especially during the Rococo period, when excess was the order of the day, the wealthy decorating their homes with elaborately hand-painted, gilded and embellished furniture. Oriental designs and lacquered finishes were prized. Overwhelmed by the demand for hand-painted objects, innovative Venetian furniture-makers developed a quicker, less expensive technique of decoration, using sheets of engravings made specifically for use in furniture decoration. They commissioned well-known artists of the day to design for them, the printed sheets being hand-coloured by apprentices before being glued to the prepared surface of a piece of furniture, or some decorative item, and lacquered many times. This method of decoration was soon adopted by private citizens who had the time required to colour, cut and lacquer. The Italian terms for découpage reflect these times: *l'arte del povero*, meaning 'poor man's art', and *lacca povera*, meaning 'poor man's lacquer'. Some découpeurs today still use engravings and hand-colour them but the majority, especially in Australia, prefer to use the beautifully coloured papers printed both here and overseas.

This Italian form of decoration soon spread to other European countries such as France, where the term for it was *découpage*, meaning 'cut-out' (from the verb *découper*, 'to cut'), which is what we call it today. It has been recorded that découpage was a hobby within the court of Marie Antoinette and that she and her ladies enjoyed cutting up original paintings by famous French artists such as Boucher, Watteau and Fragonard!

In nineteenth century England, improvements in printing saw the mass-production of sheets of coloured pictures already cut to shape, known as 'scraps'. Every subject imaginable, especially in the charming or sentimental vein, was used to decorate furniture and other objects. These decorated pieces were of the whimsical type and a far cry from the beautifully designed pieces of former times. The notable

Mrs Delaney furthered the practice of découpage with intricately cut flower miniatures. Her work can been seen today in the British Museum in London—a must-see for any keen découpeur!

Victorian England also saw cards, magazines and newspaper cuttings used as the decorative elements, on items such as hat boxes and screens. This form of découpage often included photos of family members on pieces which subsequently became family heirlooms.

Over the centuries the popularity of découpage has waxed and waned. In Italy and France, where in the eighteenth century it enjoyed such popularity, découpage has all but vanished. Fortunately, it enjoyed a resurgence in many other countries in the late twentieth century, and is once again a very popular form of decorating. In 1928 Hiram Manning and his mother Maybelle, from the United States, learnt the techniques of cutting and designing in France while staying with friends. They became avid enthusiasts and promoted and taught découpage in the United States when they returned. In 1969 Hiram Manning published a book containing photos of exquisitely cut motifs, hand-coloured, on beautifully designed objects. The modern popularity of découpage is due in part to the work of the Mannings.

Modern paints, glues, varnishes and sanding papers, and the enormous advances in colour printing and photocopying, allow the découpeurs of today to achieve beautiful and lasting work a little more easily than their forebears did—but with equal satisfaction.

Special backgrounds have long been important in découpage. Surfaces such as tortoiseshell, rosewood, mahogany and walnut timbers, marquetry, wall panelling, glass, earthenware and metal have all been decorated with designs of paper cut-outs. The simple backgrounds of earlier years were replaced, or enhanced, with more elaborate backgrounds such as gold and silver leaf and simulated lapis lazuli, malachite, marble, mother-of-pearl and alabaster surfaces. Added to these finishes was the use of shagreen paper, mulberry paper, rice paper and other exquisite hand-made papers, providing découpeurs with almost unlimited choices for backgrounds.

As with art styles in general, various countries have their own particular forms and styles of découpage reflecting their history and culture. Opportunities to see work from other countries at conventions and exhibitions can be both inspirational and motivational. Ideas for découpage designs can be culled from many sources. Art histories, the artwork of book illustrators and designers, magazines and books containing photographs of buildings and monuments, furniture and interiors, costume and jewellery, silver and metal work, ceramics and glass, can be a great inspiration for adaptation in one's own design work.

The découpaged objects on these pages decorated with artworks from around the world, reflect the diversity of styles we can draw on today for inspiration.

Four-panel Oriental screen with modern Japanese print and cherry blossoms. The background is painted gold with the room setting sketched in black.

Triptych with images from Les Très Riches Heures du Duc de Berry *(commissioned 1409). Background is gold painted over Ultramarine Blue.*

Triptych with nativity scene images flanked by cherubs and angels on the outer panels. The background is painted gold.

Gilded and oil-antiqued box découpaged with detail of Tutankhamun and his wife (c.1330 BC). The sides of the box are incised with hieroglyphs.

*Cream marbled powder bowl
with a Godward work titled*
With Violets Wreathed and
Robe of Saffron Hue *(1902).*

*Mexican box with images
from the work of Diego Rivera
(1886–1957). The
background buildings are
painted in with typical
Mexican colours.*

CHAPTER 1
Elements and principles of design

Design is a process which can be analysed into component parts. It is visual problem-solving: creating, organising and evaluating elements and principles.

The **elements** are the things we work with; the **principles** guide what we do with them. Every successful piece of design, whether it be functional or purely decorative, incorporates some or all of the design elements of variety of line, occupied and unoccupied space, positive and negative shape, colour, three-dimensional form, value and texture. The artist works to create a design by using the principles of movement, balance, repetition, contrast, emphasis and unity to make a pleasing and satisfying art form.

Design elements

How the elements are applied to an interior or an object determines the quality of a work of art. A creative designer will work thoughtfully with the materials at hand, modifying the elements according to the principles of design to achieve a satisfying and unified result.

In terms of découpage, all this comes down to choosing a well-designed item in the first place and enhancing it with a thoughtful choice of decorative motifs and decorative background. At the very simplest level, think about the elements of design as they relate to a rectangular box. Because we are not going to do an all-over coverage, we have first to choose one or more motifs appropriate to the box's intended use in shapes that complement the rectangular surface, and a background finish that complements the motif.

Assessing the appropriateness of a motif is helped by an understanding of the basic design elements. Let's consider each of the elements in turn.

OCCUPIED AND UNOCCUPIED SPACE

Space is a boundless area to which the artist gives line, shape, form, value, colour and texture. A shape occupying an area is referred to as positive space, the area around it as negative space. Links between the positive and negative space can give the illusion of depth on a two-dimensional plane or surface.

The four designs featured here are simple examples of good and bad use of space within the perimeter of the rectangle. The upper two designs do not work, while the lower two are effective uses of rectangular space. The background here is sponged (see page 67).

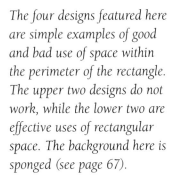

Many 'styles' and effects can be created in découpage by manipulating the cut motifs, using different sized motifs and placing them in particular ways.

- Depth is shown with overlapping shapes
- Smaller shapes give a sense of distance
- Shapes higher on the picture plane create depth or distance
- Flat shapes create the illusion of shallow space
- Outlining shapes keep them closer to the picture plane
- A plane covered with patterns eliminates any illusion of space
- Touching shapes reduce space
- Converging parallel lines suggest depth
- Colours that are warm and bright often appear to be closer to the picture plane

This vase illustrates how space can be manipulated to give the illusion of depth. The central motif is from the painting Rest *by the French artist Adolphe-William Bougereau (1825–1905). To give the illusion of wooded countryside I have created a background using sponging techniques (see page 67) combined with short brush-strokes in brown and dark green tones with copper highlights throughout. With grapevines as a decoration around the shoulder of the vase, the colour and design became united.*

- Colours that are cool or dull tend to recede into the distance

- Arrangement of lights and darks can make objects appear solid in space.

Placement of shapes cannot be left to chance. The challenge is how the space is used and being aware of the size and shape of the positive and negative spaces.

LINE

We are surrounded throughout our lives by lines of many different varieties. We see line in the branches of a tree, in the spokes of a wheel and the fronds of a fern, in the angular shapes of architecture, in the folds of our clothes and the curving slopes of hillsides. Line is like a path moving through space. It is one of the first elements called on in the creative process.

A line can be a continuous mark, which causes your eye

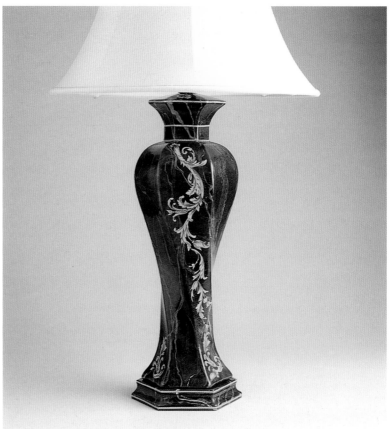

Lamp base with dark green marbled surface (see page 105). The twisted lines of the lampbase offered me the opportunity to decorate alternating sections. I created a design in which the curving lines of the floral decoration complemented the twisted shape of the base. With dominant shapes such as this, restraint in decoration is often the best option.

to follow its path. Bold, dramatic lines suggest a feeling of power. Fine, wavy, fluid lines project a feeling of sensitivity. Line may be used to create an accent or an area of interest. The designer uses line carefully to make a visual statement.

SHAPE AND FORM

Line and shape should work together in the space to be découpaged to create harmony.

Shapes can be as simple as the basic two-dimensional geometric outlines of square, rectangle, circle and triangle. Shape translated into three-dimensional volume is known as form. The five fundamental forms are the sphere, cube, cylinder, cone and pyramid. Some shapes will command more attention than others, depending on their size, colour, value, texture and detail, or their location on the picture plane. For our purposes, we just need to keep in mind that tall shapes are elevating, solid shapes appear to be stable, long flat shapes express calmness, downward shapes activate a sense of falling, while spaces between shapes can provide intriguing shapes of their own.

Vases, urns, boxes and the like are three-dimensional

objects with many different surfaces and surface directions to work on, and can provide the basis for creating an illusion with découpage.

COLOUR

In terms of physics (not a matter of serious concern here), colour is light and light is energy in motion. Colour is produced when surfaces absorb or reflect the light. Colour has several distinct visual properties: hue or tint, a colour in its purest form; value or tone, the relative lightness or darkness of a colour; and intensity, the degree of saturation of the colour.

Colours are referred to as primary, secondary and tertiary. There are also related colours, complementary colours, warm colours and cool colours. The **primary colours** are red, yellow and blue. The **secondary colours** are orange, green and violet, created by mixing the primary colours in various combinations. **Warm colours** contain more red tones and **cool colours** contain more blue tones.

This découpaged rectangular box features a painting by Veronese (1528–1588) titled The Wedding Feast at Cana. *The painting displays three-dimensional shape and form, and perspective. I have extended the tiled floor in the foreground to the edge of the box and placed pillars and urns in the foreground to create even more depth (see page 30). The colours of the tiles are duplicated on the sides. The divisions on the sides of the box contain motifs of birds, berries and flowers made of inlaid marble, a method of decorating often used in sixteenth century Italy known as 'pietre dure'.*

This plaque is découpaged with a stunning painting by Raphael entitled Virgin in the Meadow *(painted in 1505–6), a beautiful example of the use of colour. The artist used a mix of complementary colours which, when placed side by side, intensify one another. The harmony of colour is produced by the clever mixing of primary and secondary colours. A gilded frame gives a glow to the entire piece (see page 79).*

Related colours lie near each other on the colour wheel (discussed on page 29). The shades closest together are the most harmonious. A primary colour and the secondary colour which contains that primary colour, such as blue and blue-green, or blue and blue-violet, are related colours.

Complementary (or contrasting) colours lie opposite each other on the colour wheel (for example, red and green). Placed side by side they intensify each other's appearance, mixed together they produce grey.

VALUE

There is an important relationship between value, referring to the lightness or darkness of an area, and each of the other elements in a design (line, colour, texture and shape). There must be contrast between the elements and the background so the design is visible. The careful modulation of value from dark to light produces three-dimensional form, basically through the use of shading and highlighting.

For our use, the careful selection of motifs for size and colour, the shape of the area in which they will be placed and their relationship to the background space and colour must

The picture on this découpaged screen, Gerrit van Honthorst's The Concert (1624), demonstrates clever use of value by the artist, in the use of light colours for the skin and fabric in the foreground with the darker images of the interior receding into the background. This gives the painting depth and shows the relationship of value to the other elements of line, texture and shape. The painting has been extended to fill the area of the screen, using the technique discussed on page 30. The frame around the central motif has been découpaged in musical instruments and gilded, using gold and copper powder, as have the supporting cherubs and finial (see page 79).

all be considered. To do justice to the motifs there must be a good balance of light and dark so that they are not absorbed into the backgound.

TEXTURE
The final element of design, texture, is important in découpage only as implication. While texture can be perceived visually and by touch, a découpaged object's finished texture is satin-smooth. We can, however, imply texture with faux finishes of marble or wood, and invent textures, such as those created with the use of a sea sponge. I have spent many years refining background techniques which imply texture. Every project described in this book uses a different background technique to enhance the découpage.

Design principles
Having chosen a piece to decorate and considered the elements of your design, you should now think about which, if any, of those elements need to be modified by the principles of balance, movement, repetition, emphasis, contrast and unity.

On this découpaged ostrich egg, decorated with a skating scene, cut motifs combine with a painted background and crackle medium. The egg demonstrates the use of contrasting textures in the smooth brush-strokes of the snow and the use of a crackle medium on selected areas to break up the colour—this gives the impression of ice by revealing the blue base colour (see page 85).

This découpaged wall panel shows a painting in the Pre-Raphaelite tradition by John Meluish Strudwick (1849–1937), entitled Isabella. *The asymmetrical composition, with the elongated figure of the woman beside an iron stand of elegant line, makes for a very pleasing design. The background for the découpage is done in the negative dragging technique, using colours which blend with the tones of the fabric (see page 70).*

BALANCE

Balance refers to a sense of stability, when applied to opposing visual attractions or forces. In formal balance, the design elements are almost equally distributed. In other words, a composition which is divided in half so that one side is exactly or almost exactly the same as the other side is said to have symmetry. An asymmetrical design, which has neither formal balance or symmetry, can also be visually interesting and pleasing.

MOVEMENT

Movement—of forms, colours and patterns of light—should lead the eye to the area of greatest interest.

REPETITION

Repetition of common elements adds rhythm. When the intervals between the shapes are exactly the same, a formal design evolves.

Face screen (a small screen used to protect the complexion from the heat of an open fire), featuring a painting by the French artist Jacques-Louis David entitled Mars Disarmed by Venus and the Three Graces (painted 1822–24). This painting shows movement in the brewing storm as well as in the purposeful movement of the female figures. The painting's background has been extended over the entire screen using sponging techniques in matching tones (see pages 30 and 67). The edge is gilded and antiqued using cupric nitrate (see page 81).

A découpaged pedestal drop-table decorated with a repetitive collage of cherubs, flowers and fruit. The background for the design is rag rolling, using Black Japan over a gold-painted base (see page 72). The edge is gilded with Rich Gold Powder (see page 82).

EMPHASIS

Emphasis, in both a two-dimensional plane and three-dimensional form, attracts attention to important areas and creates centres of interest. A directional line moving towards the intended focus creates emphasis on that part of the design.

PROPORTION

The final consideration—and some would say the first—is unity of design, achieved in large part by the proportions into which the design surface is divided. A useful proportion when

Oval box with découpaged painting extended to the edges (see page 30), featuring Madame de Signelay and her Son with the Attributes of Thetis and Achilles *by Pierre Mignard (1691). In this painting the sight-lines of the son and angel are focused on the central figure, strengthening the emphasis created by the colour of the woman's robes and her elevated position. The blue-purple shell motifs around the base of the oval box link with the colour of the woman's robes and the shells in the painting. The sides were gilded (see page 79), then painted with Alizarine Crimson dry ground pigment mixed with shellac to create a unity of colour over the lid and base.*

dealing with rectangles, for example, is the so-called 'golden cut' or 'golden section', giving you a rectangle whose sides are in the approximate ratio of 3:2 (for example, 30 cm: 20 cm; or 18 cm: 12 cm). This ratio was sometimes used by the great masters as a starting point for achieving balance and proportion in their compositions. *The Wedding Feast at Cana*, used on the rectangular box on page 21, is a good example of the principle of proportion in action.

CHAPTER 2
Use of colour

The colour wheel

Many artists find colour wheels useful as guides to the interrelation of hue, value and intensity in designing a project. Others never touch them. Using a colour wheel can be an enjoyable exercise in reaching an understanding of how

A simple home-made colour wheel.

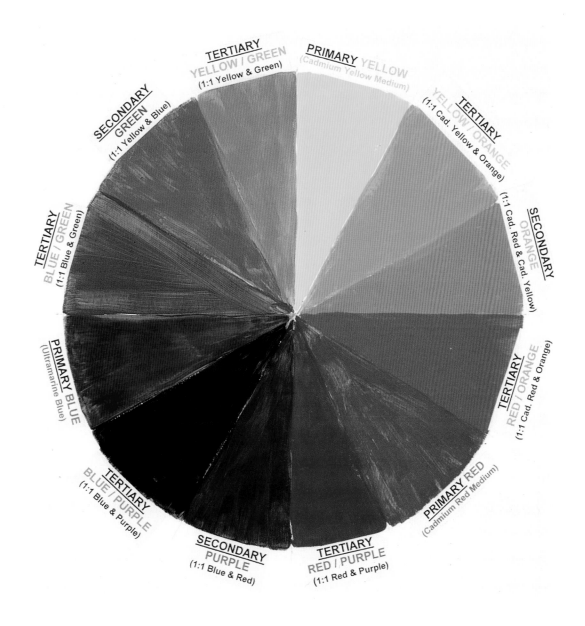

TERTIARY YELLOW / GREEN
(1:1 Yellow & Green)

PRIMARY YELLOW
(Cadmium Yellow Medium)

SECONDARY GREEN
(1:1 Yellow & Blue)

TERTIARY YELLOW / ORANGE
(1:1 Cad. Yellow & Orange)

TERTIARY BLUE / GREEN
(1:1 Blue & Green)

SECONDARY ORANGE
(1:1 Cad. Red & Cad. Yellow)

PRIMARY BLUE
(Ultramarine Blue)

TERTIARY RED / ORANGE
(1:1 Cad. Red & Orange)

TERTIARY BLUE / PURPLE
(1:1 Blue & Purple)

PRIMARY RED
(Cadmium Red Medium)

SECONDARY PURPLE
(1:1 Blue & Red)

TERTIARY RED / PURPLE
(1:1 Red & Purple)

HANDY HINT

Painting around a painting, to extend the image area, can be a great source for learning about colour from the masters. Taking a small colour copy of a fine artist's painting and extending it to cover a larger area, as shown here, can teach you more about colour identification and mixing colour than a thousand words on the subject.

- Build up sky on White using brush and sea sponge.

- Sky = Cobalt Blue + White.

- Storm clouds = Chromium Oxide Green and White over Unbleached Titanium. Lightly sponge on highlights of Unbleached Titanium.

- Trees = Burnt Umber + Chromium Oxide Green. Use Hooker's Green Deep Hue for shading. Use a shaggy short brush and a sea sponge to stipple leaves.

- Build up ground on Red Oxide.

- Foliage on ground: add brush-strokes and sponging in Burnt Umber, Yellow Oxide, Chromium Oxide Green and Hooker's Green Deep Hue.

- Shadow or darken any colours with a 1:1 mix of Ultramarine Blue + Burnt Umber.

Reproduction of A Summer Pastoral (1749) by François Boucher, with margins extended. The colours which have been identified in the painting are shown at the sides. The process is simple once the colours have been identified.

colours work together and of the infinite variety of colour in the spectrum.

A useful device for viewing the spectrum in a simplified form, a colour wheel like the one illustrated here can help you make appropriate colour choices for your project. The **primary colours** (red, yellow and blue) are equidistant on the wheel. The **secondary colours** (green, purple and orange), obtained by mixing two primary colours, are also equidistant. A **tertiary colour** is made by mixing an equal amount of a primary colour with the secondary colour next to it on the wheel. By mixing different proportions of the primary and secondary colours, a wide range of colours can be created.

Colours are related in two ways. They can contrast or harmonise. Using the colour wheel, one can see the colours which are close and in harmony and the colours which are well apart and contrasting. Colours adjoining one another on the wheel form a harmonious sequence.

The closest relationships occur between shades of the one colour, or between a primary colour and the secondary colours which contain that primary—for example, red and red-orange or red and red-purple.

The colours directly opposite one another on the wheel are contrasting partners, called complementary colours. There are three main pairs, each composed of the other two primaries: red is complementary to green, blue to orange, and yellow to purple. This relationship extends to pairs of secondary colours, so that red-orange is complementary to blue-green, blue-violet to yellow-orange, and so on. If two complementary colours of the same tone and intensity are juxtaposed, they intensify each other. The eye jumps rapidly from one colour to the other, causing an optical vibration that makes the colours shimmer.

Paints

I prefer to use Liquitex acrylic artist's colours, both high viscosity and medium viscosity, for my background finishes. Other brands,which also give excellent results, may be more readily available in your area. The Liquitex acrylic artist's colours sold in tubes are of high viscosity (a thick buttery consistency).

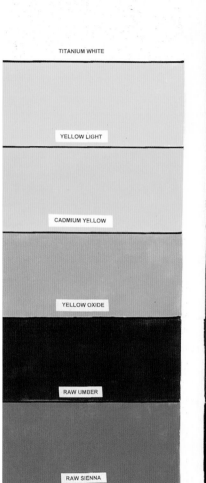

TITANIUM WHITE

CADMIUM RED

YELLOW LIGHT

DEEP MAGENTA

CADMIUM YELLOW

ULTRAMARINE BLUE

YELLOW OXIDE

PRUSSIAN BLUE

RAW UMBER

BURNT UMBER

RAW SIENNA

IVORY BLACK

Basic palette colours

COLOURS FOR A BASIC PALETTE

Titanium White

Yellow Light

Cadmium Yellow

Yellow Oxide

Raw Umber

Raw Sienna

Cadmium Red

Deep Magenta

Ultramarine Blue

Prussian Blue

Burnt Umber

Ivory Black

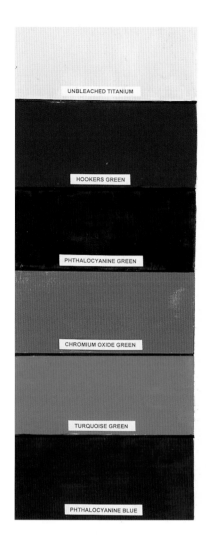

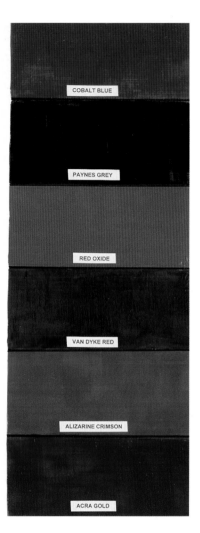

Additional colours for special effects

COLOURS FOR SPECIAL EFFECTS

Unbleached Titanium

Hookers Green

Phthalocyanine Green

Chromium Green

Turquoise Green

Phthalocyanine Blue

Cobalt Blue

Payne's Grey

Red Oxide

Van Dyke Red

Alizarine Crimson

Acra Gold

INTERFERENCE AND IRIDESCENT PAINTS

These paints obtain their colour from the presence of titanium-coated mica flakes in place of traditional pigments. They look best painted over dark opaque colours to emphasise their metallic or iridescent quality.

Iridescent colours produce a variety of metallic tones. Being optically opaque, they rely on reflected light for their effect.

Iridescent Gold

Iridescent Copper

Iridescent Bronze

Iridescent Silver

Iridescent White

Antique Gold

Antique Copper

Antique Silver

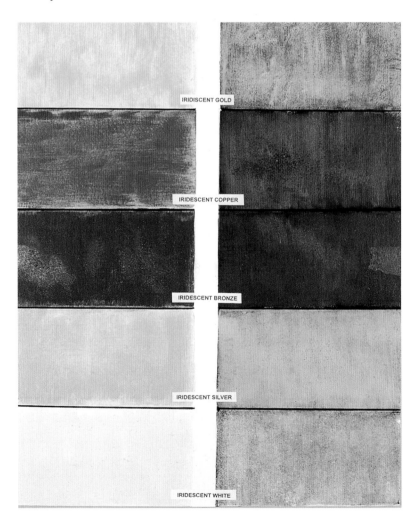

Iridescent colours over light and dark backgrounds

A large vase demonstrating the use of interference colours. It has been base-coated with a 1:1 mix of Burnt Umber and Ultramarine Blue, dried and then sponged all over with Interference Blue and dried. It was then sponged over with Interference Gold at the top, Interference Green around the centre and Interference Violet around the base (see page 67 for sponging technique).

Two gift soaps: interference colours sponged over a dark background (see page 67) highlight the dramatic découpaged images of Japanese Kabuki performers.

Sample board demonstrating the use of Interference Blue, Green, Red and Violet over dark and light backgrounds. Black is used as the background for all four colours on the left of the board. On the right, Interference Blue and Interference Green are painted over White, Interference Red and Interference Violet over a background of Parchment.

Interference pigments are colourless and transparent. On dark surfaces they produce pastel, iridescent colours of high intensity. On transparent and translucent surfaces they create shimmering visual effects due to increased light refraction.

Interference Red

Interference Orange

Interference Gold

Interference Green

Interference Blue

Interference Violet

BACKGROUND COLOURS

The following combinations using interference colours as the top coat will give some extremely interesting background effects. Dry the base colour before painting on the Interference colour.

Base colour	Top colour
1 part Raw Umber + 1 ½ parts Ultramarine Blue	Interference Green or Blue
1½ parts Deep Magenta + 1 part Cadmium Red	Interference Gold or Blue or Orange or Red
Titanium White	Interference Blue
1 part Deep Magenta + ½ part Cadmium Red	Interference White
1 part Cadmium Red + 1 part Cadmium Yellow	Interference Gold
1 part Yellow Light +½ part Prussian Blue	Interference Blue
1 part Magenta + ½ part Prussian Blue	Interference White or Gold
Parchment	Interference Orange
1 part Cadmium Yellow + ½ part White	Interference Gold

HANDY HINT

Remember many thin layers of an Interference colour rather than one thick one.

HANDY HINTS

Liquitex Acrylic Paint is produced in two viscosities: Medium Viscosity Artist Color (smooth, medium consistency) and High Viscosity Artist Color (thick and buttery consistency). I use the high viscosity paint for most of my work, especially when extending paintings. The medium viscosity is extremely useful for smooth overall background coverage because it is easily thinned with water and dries quickly. To use a paint to its best effect, you need to know some of its technical properties. The technical information given with Liquitex paints will help in your selection for a particular project.

Opacity rating The opacity (or transparency) rating of a colour is based on the characteristics of the pigments used (O = opaque, TL = translucent, TP = transparent). Reading the information on the tube will tell you if the paint will do the job you want it for. Colours which are transparent may require the application of more coats than usual to achieve satisfactory coverage. Note that some tube colours are mixes of colours which you may already have and which you could easily mix yourself and so save money—for example, Unbleached Titanium. Using a colour chart as a guide, you can mix small amounts of Raw Sienna and Raw Umber into Titanium White to get Unbleached Titanium. It pays to read the label on the tube!

Toxicity Liquitex was one of the first brands to list toxicity information for acrylic paint on the label and to identify colours chemically. Their health labelling follows American Society for Testing and Materials (ASTM) standards, and certification is given according to the Art and Craft Material Institute (ACMI). Products with a Health Label (HL) seal are certified to be properly labelled under a programme of toxicological evaluation by a medical expert.

CHAPTER 3
Techniques for découpage

Découpage means decorating an object using paper cut-outs. Découpage can be applied to almost any object which has a firm, strong, long-lasting surface—for example, wood, ceramic, metal, terracotta and glass surfaces, and objects such as boxes, furniture, screens, vases, plaques, hat boxes, cases, lamp bases and eggs.

Those who choose to do découpage often begin after seeing a beautiful piece of work in a book or at an exhibition. However one is originally introduced to découpage, the process seems to capture the imagination. I do découpage because it gives me the opportunity to use works of art from any period of history. I am constantly on the lookout for books and papers containing beautiful images, and interesting

An ex-department store mannequin purchased at an antique store provided a unique surface and shape on which to work a whimsical design incorporating butterflies, flowers and fairies. The background of the head is sponged (see page 67) and the pedestal has a red marble finish (see page 110).

shapes and surfaces on which to work. Finding something different, a unique object which has great potential as a découpage surface, brings great excitement. Care in choosing the right object is part of the chase, as is knowing when to reject those 'interesting' pieces which will require a huge amount of preparation and yet remain substandard, detracting from a beautiful design painstakingly executed.

The découpaged pieces in this book show examples of resources I have drawn on from many periods of art. The history of art is my special interest and is a never-ending source of learning and discovery.

Requirements

Many of the requirements for découpage are easy to find, but some must be sourced from suppliers who specialise in art and craft products. There are many excellent suppliers who will gladly mail out products. Some are listed at the end of this book. I have listed first the items which are essential; as you become more involved you will gradually build up a greater variety of paints and mediums.

A room or studio which can be dedicated to your efforts is the ideal place to work in, but any light, airy, dust-free space with a table and chair and some storage cupboards will suffice. Easy access to a tap and sink is also necessary. Looking after yourself is important, so use disposable gloves to protect the skin when painting and varnishing, a dust mask when sanding and a fume mask when varnishing. Also, remember to be friendly to the environment—don't pour leftover paint and other liquids into the drain, but dispose of them as you would any poisonous substance. Caring for your equipment, by adhering to the manufacturer's instructions for storing paints and mediums, cleaning and storing brushes and protecting scissors, makes economic sense.

ESSENTIALS

(items marked * are available from découpage suppliers and craft stores)

1. Prints of pictures, coloured or black and white, can be sourced from wrapping paper, calendars, good quality photocopies from art books (can be used on items for personal use only, not on items for sale), cards, magazines, fabric or hand-coloured prints

2. Scissors*—sharp, curved, with a fine point (cuticle or iris scissors) or a blade knife

3. Brayer* (roller for pressing images down)

4. Artist's acrylic paints—Liquitex tubes, jars and specialty colours as listed on page 33, or other good quality artist's acrylics

5. Mediums*—Liquitex Gloss Medium and Varnish, scumble and Crackle Medium

6. Brushes*:
   Nos 3, 6, 12, round and flat synthetics
   000 rigger (long, flexible hair)
   Nos 3, 6 filberts (curved at the tip)
   short stiff bristle brush for textural effects
   long flat brush for gluing
   short flat, soft brush for varnishing
   palette knife

7. White palette (large if a lot of mixing is required)

8. Sea sponges*—round, flat, with both small and large pores

9. Glues*—Liquitex Gloss Medium and Varnish (GMV), wallpaper paste, PVA glue, craft glue

10. Varnishes—oil-based and water-based

11. Protective mask and goggles

12. Sandpapers:
    600, 800, 1200 and 2000 wet/dry (used wet for hand-sanding)
    320 silicon carbide velour for hand-sanding
    3-pack single-sided sanding pads (fine, ultra-fine and superfine) for electric sander
    120, 240, 320, 400 velour-backed for electric sander

13. Electric sander is optional

14. Micro-Mesh Polishing Kit*

15. Blu-tack

ACCESSORIES

Blade knife and self-mending cutting pad

Water-soluble coloured pencils

Masking tape

Gilding leaf and size (glue)

Cotton buds

Disposable gloves

Cotton gloves

Sandpaper, 240 garnet

Liquitex Color Mixing chart

Chamois

Tack cloth

Cotton cloths

Sketch pad

HB pencil

Butcher's paper/newsprint

Polish, e.g. Liberon Burnishing Cream or Clear Wax

Timber filler

Spackle/plaster filler

Kitchen sponges cut into smaller pieces

Water containers

Ruler

Spirit level

Tweezers

Non-stick paper (Glad Bake)

Preparation

It is of paramount importance to properly prepare the surface of any object to be découpaged. The quality of the finished work will only be as good as the quality of the preparation. Many hours will be spent painting, cutting, designing, varnishing and sanding to achieve the effect you are looking for, and any imperfections in the preparation of the surface will detract from the final result. The outcome of good preparation is an object with a smooth, sealed surface on which you can confidently paint the background colour and glue the images.

Materials

Sandpaper

Timber filler

Spackle/plaster filler

Varnish stripper

Brushes for sealing

Liquitex Gloss Medium and Varnish (GMV)

Gesso or Magic Effects Special Paint (a Jennifer Bennell plaster-based product)

Background artist's colours

Cloths

000 steel wool

Scouring pads

Turpentine

Water

Skewers for holding eggs

Process

Whatever the object, it must be cleaned, filled, sanded and sealed on the inside, as well as on the outside, for the best result. Fill all gaps and indentations, using a timber filler for wood or plaster filler for ceramics. Sand with a scouring pad, sandpaper or steel wool. Clean the surface of all dust, using a brush first, then a tack cloth.

New timber or craftwood can be sealed with either GMV, gesso or Magic Effects Special Paint. From two to four coats may be necessary to achieve a good smooth surface, depending on the type of timber. Sand between each coat.

Old or varnished timber has to be cleaned of any oil-based products, which are removed by sanding or stripping, then sealed with GMV or gesso.

Ceramics are naturally porous. If they are not fully glazed, on the inside and the base, they must be sealed with a water-based varnish. Swirl the varnish around the inside and upend the item to drain. Seal the outside and the base with gesso or artist's colours. The outside must then be painted with at least two coats of artist's colours as a base-coat to complement the images being used. Alternatively, paint on a special surface effect undercoat, following the instructions in Chapter 5.

Glossy surfaces such as plastic or glazed ceramic are too slick for paint and glue to adhere to if left untreated. A bonding medium must be applied to give a 'key' or 'grip' to the surface. After the medium is applied, seal with gesso, checking the manufacturer's instructions for any special hints.

Metal objects must be thoroughly cleaned of any rust and grime. Sandblasting may be needed to remove built-up paint layers on older pieces. Clean off any grease with sugar soap.

Sand the surface to provide a 'grip' or 'key' for painting and gluing.

Eggs can be prepared by washing in a 1:1 solution of water and white vinegar to remove any grease. If the uneven surface characteristic of ostrich and emu eggs is not desired as an element of the finished work, apply about four coats of gesso (or Magic Effects Special Paint) and sand smooth. Apply the background colour to the sanded surface. Support the egg on a skewer held in a bottle filled with rice or scrunched-up paper.

Background effects

While the cut image is the highlight of the work, the right background, chosen from the finishes in Chapters 4 and 5, is vital to the overall finished result. The colours of the image you have chosen will dictate the finish you use, the colours, their tones and values. It is essential to use colours which contrast with, and complement, the image. Experiment with a sample board painted with the colour combinations you think best suit the image, and make adjustments as need be. Lay the cut-out images on the sample board to see if you are getting the effect you want, remembering that some colours dominate others, and that colour intensity can appear to change in different lighting conditions.

HANDY HINT

Don't be afraid to mix lots of different colour combinations—be daring with the paint. Use a colour wheel or a Liquitex Mixing Guide to find complementary colour relationships for an image. The colours should either contrast or harmonise. After making sample boards of the colours, go away from the work for a while. When you look at it later you might have a better idea. Again, if in doubt, ask for a second opinion.

Train your eye to view colour combinations everywhere. Nature, buildings, fashions, theatre costumes and scenery, television advertisements, movies—everything you come in contact with may provide a potential colour combination. Develop a critical eye for colour. Try to always use correct colour names, for both the colours from the colour wheel and the paints you use. This will consolidate your colour knowledge and also give you confidence when identifying colours.

Special background effects can provide very interesting

contrasts for your découpage images. To know just which is the right special effect to match an image takes time, so experiment first. The right brush-stroke or texture can be very simple to apply and provide a unique background. If the images you are using are very detailed or 'busy', be careful that the background colour or effect does not compete with and detract from the cut-outs. Remember—the cut image is the highlight of the work!

The motifs—assembling and cutting

Finding just the right image for a special object can be a mission in itself. It can sometimes take months to locate the perfect picture! You will find that over time you develop a 'nose' for appropriate resources.

Every available paper product is a potential source of images. Remember, however, that you must use images printed only on good quality paper. If you are in love with something on poor quality paper, have a good colour photocopy made. Specialist outlets for découpage supplies are an invaluable source of images, as they import beautiful papers and tap into every source known to keep up the supply to hungry découpeurs. (See the suppliers list on page 139.) Fellow découpeurs can also be of great assistance in finding that elusive image.

Colour photocopies of fabrics, photographs, magazine pictures and artworks can be copied, enlarged, reduced or reversed to make personalised designs.

Keep copyright laws in mind when making photocopies. Remember—items for sale must be made with images free of copyright restrictions.

HANDY HINT

Storing resources such as borders, portraits for focal images, geometric, floral and art period images can make the task of finding the right image for a project much easier. A folder of both cut and uncut material can save you valuable time. Filing images according to art period or style, borders, geometrics, portraits or your own area of interest is a good organisational strategy.

All images on porous paper, or any paper of poorer quality, need to be sealed with GMV to protect them before you start cutting. This is to prevent varnish soaking through the paper and discolouring the image or, even worse, lifting the image from the surface. Some découpeurs also prefer to seal photocopies as the firm massaging action used when gluing on the image can sometimes lift the colour. If in doubt—seal.

HANDY HINT

Use photocopy machines which produce high-quality copies, and photocopy operators who are sympathetic to your needs!

Cutting out your découpage images is a lot more exacting a task than you might imagine. It is a skill which requires a great deal of concentration and needs to be practised for short periods in the beginning and perfected over a longer period.

Begin with larger images and graduate to fine detailed cutting when you feel more confident. Cut only manageable-sized pieces of paper. Large pieces of paper can get in the way of the scissors, twisting around and turning back on themselves, and making your cutting irregular. Working with smaller pieces which can be glued and joined together later is a practical way of dealing with larger resources.

Always cut inner areas first and outer lines second. Right-handed cutters work in an anti-clockwise direction around the outside edge of an image, and clockwise on inner areas. Left-handed cutters cut in a clockwise direction around the outside edge, and anti-clockwise on inner areas.

Right-handed cutters should hold the paper loosely in the left hand, ready to turn it when necessary. The right elbow should remain rested at the hip with the curved scissor blades constantly at an angle turned away from the image. Cutting at an angle produces a desirable bevelled edge, which is lower to the surface than a blunt straight edge when glued down.

Cut away the enclosed inner areas first in a clockwise direction, then the outside of the image, in an anti-clockwise direction. This way the bulk of the image will always be on the left-hand side, which makes cutting easier. Left-handed cutters should reverse these directions, and cut anti-clockwise within enclosed areas and clockwise around the outer edge.

Use the very tips of the blades in a nibbling action.

Turning the paper, not the scissors, will produce smooth, even cutting.

Cut right on the line of the image, doing any perfecting of unclear lines as you go. It is almost impossible later on to accurately clean up the edges of a strip of paper only ⅛ inch (2 mm) wide.

To cut images with crossed-over or enclosed areas, such as you will often find in vines or bouquets of flowers, where the background has to be cut away, pierce the paper with the tips of the scissors, then come up through the hole with one blade to begin cutting.

Quite often, as the cut images are completed and the design unfolds before you, you will find that many more cut images are required than you first expected. This is par for the course. If you find you have surplus images for a particular project, however, don't throw them out, but file them away for later use. Don't waste cut images!

Images cut from thicker paper will often have obvious white edges. These can be coloured in a sepia tone with a moistened coloured pencil, a paintbrush dipped into a similar colour, or a felt-tipped pen, to make them less obvious.

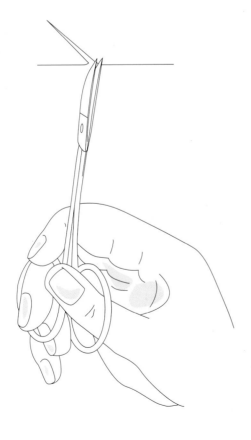

Scissors held with the right hand slightly twisted away from the body. The curved tips of the blades are pointing outwards from the paper and cutting with only the tips of the blades. The angle of cut is shown in the cross-section, showing the bevelled edge resulting from holding the scissors at this angle.

HANDY HINT

To check that a design really works, make a template based on the cut-outs, and lay it over the surface of the object to be decorated. Some découpeurs like to Blu-tack the images directly onto the object, especially when they are dealing with curved surfaces. To help get the images in the right place when you are gluing them down, draw a rough sketch of where each piece is to go. It is often a good idea to lay out the design and just leave things alone for a while. A few hours break may make any design flaws obvious. Ask for a second opinion if in doubt.

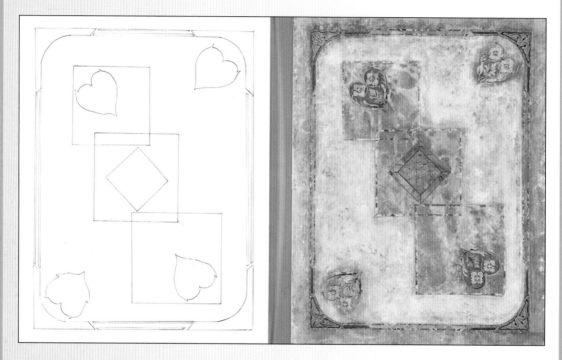

Left: Template of découpage design. Right: Design based on template

Gluing and sealing the images

If the design is a complicated one, make a template of it, using the cut-out images. This will lessen the risk of gluing down the images in the wrong place. If the design is laid out beside the object to be worked on, and the pieces are ready to pick up and position as needed, the design will go into place as planned. Complicated or detailed cut-outs should be glued down in small pieces. Gluing down the cut-outs in sections keeps the process organised so if interruptions occur it is easy to continue at a later date. After gluing down all images and cleaning the surface, the entire object must be sealed with at least four coats of GMV—but not until the glue has dried.

This helps protect the paper cut-outs and build up the surface level before the varnishing begins.

The type of paper and the size of the image will determine what type of glue should be used. If in doubt, use a scrap of the waste paper cut from the work to test the glue first. Some papers may stretch and others shrink when glue is applied, or as it dries. Every découpeur has favourite glues which work well for them. Experimenting with the various glues available (and experience) will help you decide which glue is appropriate for a certain project.

Materials

Gloss Medium and Varnish (GMV)

Good quality wallpaper paste

Clear craft glue for foil or metal papers

Gluing brushes—soft haired, 1 inch (2.5 cm) brush for large areas, smaller brushes for small areas

Brayer (to press down images)

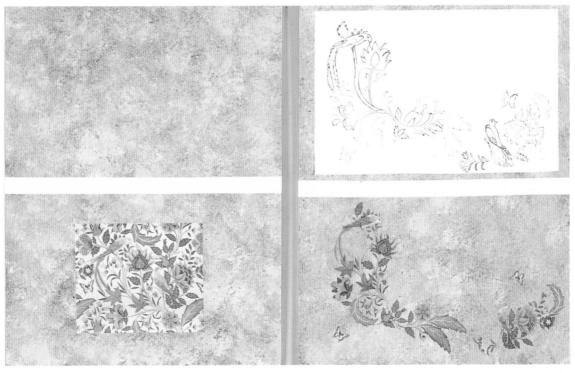

The découpage process. Above left: Sponged background with base colour Hooker's Deep Green Hue sponged with Yellow Oxide and White. Below left: Wrapping paper with images for cutting. Above right: Template of design using birds, flowers and butterflies. Below right: Motifs cut, placed and glued following the template. Background and motifs sealed with four coats of GMV, ready for varnishing.

Kitchen sponges, large and small (for cleaning off glue)

Blade knife or scalpel and self-mending cutting pad

Water basin

Cloths

Tweezers (for moving around tiny pieces of paper)

White vinegar

HANDY HINT

The rules of thumb for deciding which glues should be used are:

- Larger pictures—wallpaper paste
- Smaller pictures and finely cut paper—GMV
- Foils—good quality clear craft glue

WALLPAPER PASTE

A good quality wallpaper paste, mixed to a gel consistency with no lumps, is very easy to use and is my preferred option for larger images, as it is fairly slow-drying and allows time to move and reposition images.

Brush a generous amount of paste onto the surface where the image is to go. Gently lay the image over the glue. Brush glue onto the face of the image as well to make massaging it into place easier. Using the glue brush, or your hand, press down the image, working from the centre to the outer edges. Now, using the palm of the hand, or the side of your fisted hand, massage gently from the centre of the image out to the edges to remove any air bubbles.

Wipe over the surface of the image with a damp kitchen sponge to remove any surplus glue. Any glue on the surface of the object should also be removed at this stage. Roll the brayer over the image to flatten the image and squeeze out excess glue. Work from the centre to the edges, working gently so you don't remove all the glue. After each roll, wipe away any glue from the surface of the brayer. Dry glue can be removed from the surface of the image with a 1:1 mix of water and white vinegar. Leave overnight or longer, depending on drying conditions, before sealing with 4 coats of GMV prior to varnishing.

GLOSS MEDIUM AND VARNISH

Gloss Medium and Varnish (GMV) is a very fast-drying glue. It is essential to work quickly and avoid interruptions. (Phone disconnected for this!)

When using GMV on small cut-outs, brush enough glue onto the surface area to match the size of the image and brush down the cut-out with the GMV-coated brush. Press down the image by massaging gently from the centre out to the edges, first with your fingers, then with a damp sponge, changing the sponge frequently for a clean one. Use the brayer only if absolutely necessary. With cut-outs of border strips, work in short sections, brushing on just enough glue to lay down 1–2 inches (2–5 cm) of border at a time. Clean around the cut-outs with a damp sponge.

If you are using GMV on a larger picture, it is essential to brush the GMV onto the entire area that the image will cover. Then, working from the centre out to the edges, quickly massage the picture into place with the brush containing GMV, then the clean brayer. Wipe over the image and the surrounding area with a damp sponge to remove any GMV. Use a 1:1 water and vinegar solution to remove any dried glue. Leave for a few hours or overnight before sealing with 4 coats of GMV prior to varnishing.

PVA GLUE

PVA glue (Aquadhere) can be used on glass. First ensure the glass is thoroughly clean, washing it in warm soapy water and rinsing in a 1:1 solution of water and white vinegar. On the top surface of the glass mark where the image is to be positioned, using a felt pen. Paint the coloured side of the image with a generous amount of glue and position it on the undersurface of the glass, using the felt pen marks as a guide. The picture is then gently massaged into place, working from the middle of the image to the outer edge, using a wet finger as the massaging tool.

Great care must be taken to remove any air bubbles, which will be visible through the glass when the glue dries. Keep massaging the bubbles with wet fingers and wipe the glue off with a damp sponge. This process takes time but it is very important to remove all air bubbles.

Use cotton buds or similar to wipe away glue from the edge of the images. Clean the surrounding area of glass with a damp sponge, being careful not to get water under the paper. Any dry glue on the glass can be removed with the mixture of vinegar and water.

Glue can sometimes take days to dry on glass. The object must be left until the glue is clear. The surface can then be painted with a background colour or other paper images applied using the same process. Leave for a few days or longer, depending on drying conditions, before sealing with 4 coats of GMV prior to varnishing.

AIR BUBBLES

Air bubbles are a serious concern in découpage. Wherever bubbles are left under an image, the image will lift from the surface when varnish is applied. After gluing down an image, hold the work up to a good light to see if any raised areas are visible. Press the raised area with a finger. If it feels hollow, or moves up and down, an air bubble is the likely cause. Sometimes spots of thick, uneven glue can be mistaken for air bubbles, but in this case, when the glue dries the surface will even out.

HANDY HINT

To eliminate air bubbles which show up when the glue has dried, follow these guidelines. With a very sharp scalpel, cut along a line of the image close to the edge of the bubble, and lift up the paper. Brush GMV glue under the lifted area, then press down the paper, clean the area with a damp sponge and reseal the surface with GMV. Also use GMV to eliminate bubbles appearing when wallpaper paste is used.

Varnishing

Before you varnish your project, the entire surface must be sealed with four coats of GMV. You now need to select the varnish best suited for the project, bearing in mind the materials used for the background finish. You need to be certain that the varnish you use will enhance your work without changing the colour of the images and your original concept.

It is important to remember that oil-based products will safely go over water-based products, but you can never use water-based products over oil. If oil paints have been used in the surface finish, an oil-based varnish will be required. Always check the varnish label before use.

Many varnishes, particularly oil-based ones, will affect the colour of the images and the painted background. If the degree of change is undesirable, choose a different varnish. It must be recognised, however, that because so many coats of varnish are used, some colour change is inevitable, even though sanding cuts back the depth. It is virtually impossible

Découpage under glass, featuring a Chinese painting delightfully titled The Cap and Sash of an Official Are Handed Down from Generation to Generation: Your Son Certainly Will Enjoy a Brilliant Career *(The Hermitage). Textured hand-made Japanese paper was used behind the picture, with interference colours painted under and over the textured paper to match the pale colours of the motif (see page 37). The edge of the plate is gilded using Rich Gold Powder.*

for the varnishing process to have no effect on colour. Oil-based varnishes will put an amber glow over the work; some others may give a plastic look.

HANDY HINT

Make up some varnish testers, individual pieces of glass coated with about five coats of various varnishes, and labelled for identification. Placing them over your work will give a fair indication of how the finished piece will be affected.

Because of the vast number of varnish products available, it is impossible to claim that any one is 'the best'. Experience is the best guide. People have had success with certain brands under certain conditions for certain projects. The ease of applying a product and the speed with which it dries, as well as ease of sanding, are the main factors behind most découpeurs' choice of varnish.

Choice of varnish will be governed by:

1. Climate—is it hot, dry, humid, wet, windy? Ideal conditions are medium temperature with a light breeze. Humid conditions are the worst to work under and should be avoided.

2. The effect the varnish will have on the colours used on the background and the images.

3. Access to a space which is well ventilated and dust-free.

4. The health of the person and others in the immediate environment.

5. The mediums used on the background—are they water-based or oil-based?

6. Ease of application.

7. Speed of drying.

8. Ease of sanding.

9. Ease of polishing.

The desired outcome for varnishing over découpage is a clear, smooth, unblemished surface which enhances the work.

Materials

Varnish—I have had success with Feast Watson Weatherproof (oil-based), Cabot's Gelclear (oil-based), Cabot's Clear Floor (water-based)

Varnishing brush, 1 inch (2.5 cm) nylon/Taklon

Turpentine (for cleaning up oil-based varnish)

Jar of turpentine for cleaning brush used in oil-based varnish

Tack cloth

Small kitchen sponges for wiping drips, cleaning edges

Carbon mask or respirator

Disposable gloves

Spirit level

Level bench at which to work

Lazy Susan for turning work

Non-stick paper (Glad Bake)

HANDY HINTS

For achieving a good surface finish the conditions under which you work are important.

- A clean, dust-free environment, with cross-ventilation, is essential.

- A good-quality varnish and varnishing brush will lessen the likelihood of brush-marks.

- A carbon mask and protective gloves are essential for maintaining good health as fumes from both kinds of varnish can be harmful.

FLAT SURFACES

Brush method

The first step is to disconnect the phone! Interruptions will spoil your work.

Varnishing a two-dimensional object, like a flat box lid or a screen, is a straightforward process. Sit it above the bench on a sturdy support, using a small spirit level to check that it is balanced and level. Gently dust down the entire area to be varnished with a tack cloth to remove dust particles.

HANDY HINT

Some varnishes require stirring and others do not. Read the instructions on the label.

Dip the brush into the varnish, halfway up to the ferrule (the metal clasp holding the hairs) but never into the ferrule. The brush must be fully loaded with varnish and taken to the work. Place it at the top edge of the object 3/8 inch (1 cm) in from the left-hand side. (I'm assuming you're right-handed like me!) Hold the brush gently at a 45-degree angle and, without pressing, paint the varnish onto the surface parallel to the top edge. Returning to the left-hand side, this time starting at the very edge, brush over the same line to spread the varnish over that line evenly. Be careful not go too close to the edge and cause runs. Take the next line of varnish across the surface in the same manner, overlapping the previous line a little. Continue working quickly and methodically, applying line after line without stopping until the entire surface is covered. Clean the brush when you have finished, as dried varnish will ruin it.

Keep a record of the number of coats of varnish applied, showing brush direction and the date of application.

The timing of the next application depends on the varnish used, the suggested drying time between coats, temperature and humidity levels. Each subsequent coat should be made in a different direction to the previous one—if the first coat is worked from left to right, the next one should be worked from right to left, the third one from top to bottom, the fourth from bottom to top. This cycle is repeated until the varnished surface has been built up sufficiently to protect the images before sanding begins. This often means about twenty coats.

Each surface of a three-dimensional flat object, like a box, must be varnished and left horizontal to dry before proceeding with the next face. This will help to eliminate varnish runs. Turn to the next face of the box and, as each surface dries, keep turning it to varnish the next face. This way each face of the box has the same number of coats of varnish.

Flooding method

Once a few coats of varnish have been brushed on, forming a protective layer over the motifs, you can switch to flooding, in which a very thick layer of varnish is applied to an object resting horizontally and perfectly level. Check again with the spirit level. Lay foil under the support to collect the varnish run-off. Very good lighting is essential so that no skipped areas occur, and weather conditions must be perfect.

This thick application is gently poured from a jug, using a brush to assist the flow and spread the varnish evenly. After varnish has been applied to the entire area, take the brush across the surface in long sweeps to ensure even coverage. As the layer is finished, check for any dribbles down the edges of the work and wipe them off with a damp sponge to avoid unsightly build-up. Clean the brush now as dried varnish will ruin the bristles.

A flooded layer of varnish takes much longer to dry because of its thickness, and thus has to be left for many days. If another layer is applied too soon, onto sticky varnish, wrinkling will occur. Varnish which 'withers' to resemble crocodile skin or orange peel means the previous layer has not dried.

The number of coats of varnish required on a particular project will depend partly on how high the paper images stand away from the surface. Where overlapping images have been used they will stand even higher. The number of coats will also depend on the consistency of the varnish. A rule of thumb is at least fifteen to twenty coats of varnish of a thinner consistency, and ten to twelve coats of a varnish of thicker consistency.

HANDY HINTS

- Do not touch the wet surface with your fingers, or be tempted to rebrush, because drying will begin almost immediately—this is critical.

- Leave the varnished work to dry in a dust-free, cross-ventilated place, out of direct sunlight.

- Before each application of varnish, wipe the tack cloth gently over the surface to remove any dust particles.

- Climatic conditions can affect estimated drying times. Do not be tempted to apply another layer of varnish too soon.

CURVED SURFACES

Vases and other upright objects

Using a fully loaded brush, brush the varnish on in the four-direction cycle described on page 55, working from the top to the base and from the base to the top, then around the object both clockwise and anti-clockwise. (Waiting until each coat has fully dried of course!) Depending on the shape and contour of the object, the choice of place to begin varnishing is made with regard to how manageable the flow of the varnish will be.

A vase which is slender at the top and bulging towards the base will require less varnish on the brush to cover the surface area at the top and more to cover the bulge near the base. Work with a fully loaded brush when varnishing the larger part and a partly loaded brush at the smaller part.

HANDY HINT

Rounded items are easier to varnish if set in the centre of a rotating board like a lazy Susan, or a potter's wheel.

EGGS

A small egg can be varnished by simply dipping the whole egg into a container of varnish which is large enough to hold the egg and with enough space in the container to displace the varnish. The dipping method uses much more varnish than painting but is very easy and produces a surface free from brush-strokes.

Glue a little piece of paper which matches the finished colour over the hole in the egg. When the glue is dry, gently push a support stick through the paper, long enough to reach the top of the egg. Use Blu-tack to secure the support stick in place. Dip the egg into the varnish at an angle, deep enough to meet the hole where the stick enters. Gently turn once from side to side to make sure the egg is completely covered with varnish. Slowly withdraw the egg from the varnish and hold upside down over the container until drops of varnish begin to fall. Upturn the egg on the stick and place it into a jar filled with rice or crumpled foil or paper, where the excess varnish which runs down the stick can collect. Leave the egg on the stick to dry between dippings.

Larger eggs can be prepared with a stick support in the same way. If you do not have a large enough container to dip the egg, it can be stood upright on the support and the varnish brushed on in the usual manner.

HANDY HINT

After dipping the egg into the varnish, various sized eggs can be supported on a heavy, flat piece of timber in which holes have been drilled to hold the support sticks. The timber is placed into a foil tray to collect the surplus varnish.

HANDY HINTS

Cleaning the brushes which are used for varnishing is a very important part of the varnishing process. A good quality brush is expensive and unclogged hairs promote smooth, even brush-strokes.

- Keep separate brushes for oil-based and water-based varnishes.

- When you are working with an **oil-based varnish**, between applications suspend the brush in a container of turpentine, using a peg clasped to the brush's wooden handle. Wipe the brush lightly onto a paper towel before the next use.

- Renew the turpentine each week to avoid clogged bristles and contamination of the brush with old turpentine.

- When you are working with a **water-based varnish**, between applications clean the brush in water and brush-cleaner and stand upright to dry on the tip of the handle.

- If you are varnishing frequently you could leave the brush suspended by a peg in a jar of clean water between projects.

Sanding

The process of sanding can be tedious, but with perseverance a beautiful piece of découpage will be produced. Good sanding will make the difference between an ordinary work and an extraordinary one!

Materials

Dust mask (always use when dry sanding)

Tack cloth

Cork sanding block

Small hand-held sanding machine (optional)

Abrasive restorer (to clean sandpaper)

Silicon carbide abrasive sheets for hand-sanding both oil-based and water-based varnish:

240, 320 and 400 dry

600, 800, 1200, 2000, 2500 wet-and-dry

Velour-backed abrasive sheets #120, #240, #320, #400 for electric sanding:

single-sided (3-pack) sanding pads, fine, ultra fine and super fine (my personal choice)

Micro-Mesh kit for wet hand-sanding:

foam block, Micro-Mesh sheets #1500, #2400, #4000, #6000, #8000, #12000 (used for the final polishing and gives a brilliant sheen to the work)

Towel

Clean rags

Process

Sanding is best done out of doors and away from the area where you do your varnishing. A stable table on which to work will assist in keeping the sanding even.

Dry sanding Place the work to be sanded on a thick layer of newspaper covered with a towel or cloth, and have at hand clean dry cloths to wipe away the dust. Always use a dust mask when dry sanding.

Wet sanding Place the work on thick towels, and do the sanding near a water source because the object must be kept wet throughout the sanding process. Have cloths at hand to wipe off the sludge. Keep the sandpaper clean by washing.

Hand sanding Work with a firm even pressure, either in a circular motion or from left to right in straight lines. It is necessary to work consistently and in small areas at a time, working over the piece methodically. Keep the sandpaper clean by brushing off the grit regularly.

Hand-held sanding machine A small machine is of great assistance for dry sanding and reduces greatly the time spent on the work. Care should be taken to rest the motor periodically and check the cleanliness of the sandpaper. Clean the sandpaper on an abrasive restorer to maximise its use. The three-pack sanding pads can be stretched over smaller sanding machines and are very effective used in this way.

After sufficient coats of varnish have been applied (from 15 to 20, depending on the thickness of the varnish), and only when the varnish is thoroughly dry, can sanding begin. If any thick runs and uneven areas have appeared, a coarse abrasive pad will be required to cut back the build-up to the general level. Suitable sandpapers here are Siacar 320 or the fine-grade sanding pad used on an electric sander (very useful at this stage). Gradually work over the uneven areas until the surface is reasonably smooth, then, using the various grades of paper from coarse to fine, sand carefully over the images until the surface becomes level and smooth.

Take great care not to over-sand, as you risk cutting through to the paper images. If this does happen, stop sanding immediately and touch up the paper with a paint colour to blend in with the image. Seal the painted area with GMV. When the GMV is dry, clean the surface thoroughly and continue the varnishing process. If the images are damaged, it means that insufficient varnish has been applied. Enough extra coats will be required to bring the level of the surface perfectly even, with no indentations or varying levels around the images.

The sanding process is repeated after every two to three coats of varnish.

Occasionally, once the surface is perfectly even and all bumps and runs have been sanded away, a 'watermark' area (which looks like a wavy pattern in the varnish) may appear on the surface. This must be eliminated before the final polishing can be done. Paint over any watermarks with two or three coats of a good-quality varnish to provide a smooth surface before polishing.

Some découpeurs use a fresh tin of varnish for the final three coats as a matter of course. On bisque or timber, three final coats of marine varnish will give a good surface for polishing.

Polishing

The varnished object must be cured (left to 'set') for a month before polishing. This is essential to allow the varnish to harden sufficiently.

The three-pack, single-sided sanding pads, obtainable from specialist découpeur suppliers, have proven to be an excellent polishing tool as well as a sanding tool. They give a beautiful marble-smooth finish and are my preferred method, allowing sanding and polishing in one action.

Once the desired finish has been achieved with the sanding pads, the next step in finishing is simply to use a good liquid furniture polish, car polish or clear wax. Alternatively, you can use a Micro-Mesh kit, generally beginning with the lowest numbered grade, although if the surface is perfectly smooth, starting with a higher number will be appropriate. Follow carefully the manufacturer's instructions given in the kit. Work up to the highest number if an absolutely brilliant sheen is required. This gives a highly polished finished second to none, and is the way I like to finish my work. Some people prefer to stop a little before this point because a matt finish is desired. No further waxing or liquid polish is required.

Maintenance

Découpage finished with a Micro-Mesh kit is maintained by simply wiping over with a damp cloth. Most of the pieces featured in this book have been polished with the Micro-Mesh system—for example, the box on page 21, the face screen on page 26 and the granite oval box on page 115.

To maintain a beautiful finish on découpage originally polished without the Micro-Mesh kit, wipe over with a damp cloth to remove any dust and polish with a liquid polish such as Liberon Burnishing Cream.

Keeping découpage out of direct sunlight is essential for the life of the work. Direct sunlight will cause the colours on the printed images to fade, and eventually discolour the varnish.

CHAPTER 4
Basic surface techniques

Top left: Small side-table featuring the negative dragging technique (see page 70) as background for a repetitive Art Nouveau design.

Left: A box demonstrating the single-process bagging technique on the sides (see page 73). The lid features a painting by John Duncan titled Tristan and Isolde *(1912) which has been painted to extend to the edges (see page 30).*

A lamp base with a rag-rolled finish (gold base coat and black Japan glaze) to tone with the motifs used in the design (see page 72).

The three pictures demonstrate some of the techniques treated in this chapter. The instructions I give here are basic techniques for achieving textures and effects on both small and large surfaces. The techniques can be adapted to suit a variety of needs and can be varied by choice of paint colours and mediums. The results can be works both stunning and unique.

When applying any of these finishes, it is important that you prepare the surface well, ensuring that it is clean, sanded and undercoated. Two to five coats of gesso, Magic Effects Special Paint or interior undercoat give a good working surface. Make sure the product you choose for surface preparation is compatible with the paints and mediums to be used in the technique (work up a test board if you are not certain).

Whatever technique you are going to use, I recommend that you work up a sample before you attempt the final thing. Practice is necessary to achieve these effects, as it takes time to develop the correct technique for using the 'tools' for each finish. Mixing adequate amounts of colour for the area to be worked on, before you start, is also important (this is one time where too much is definitely better than too little, even if you have to throw out the excess).

Climatic conditions play an important role in drying times, so judgements should be made accordingly.

All basic techniques for creating special surface effects must be practised. It is essential that you do this with the simple tools that each technique requires.

Checklist

- All surface areas to be painted with a special effect should be prepared by cleaning, filling, sanding and sealing.

- Unless otherwise stated, in the following instructions 'glaze' means a mix of 1 part paint + 1 part scumble + 1 part water.

- Remember scumble medium retards drying time so the glaze mixture will take much longer to dry than paint.

- 'Artist's acrylic paints' and 'Gloss Medium and Varnish (GMV)' refer to the Liquitex brand unless otherwise stated. Larger areas may require the use of interior house paint, which can be colour-matched using a Liquitex Color Guide.

- Mediums used are Liquitex, Magic Effects, Jo Sonja's and Langridge products.

- If you are using gesso or Magic Effects Special Paint as the undercoat/sealer, remember these are porous paints which absorb glues and some mediums. You will have to further seal these products with a non-porous paint or medium or first test the area to be worked. Gesso is intended for small areas or objects of découpage, not larger surfaces such as walls.

- Eliminate brush-strokes in gesso or paint by mixing with water to thin out the paint, or by stippling lightly with a brush or fine damp sponge. The use of medium viscosity paint will result in less brush-marks and subsequently a smoother finish.

- All textured surfaces can be sealed with varnish if desired.

Sponging

Sponging, the first of the basic techniques, is used on many occasions to create various effects. Hold the sea sponge gently in the palm of the hand without squeezing. A sideways rolling action rather than a dabbing action will result in a more natural appearance. Sponging can be done both positively and negatively.

Materials

Sealer: either GMV, gesso, Magic Effects Special Paint or interior undercoat

Artist's acrylics or interior house paints in two contrasting colours (one forms the background, the other is mixed as a glaze)

GMV

Brushes

Sea sponge

Scumble medium

Butcher's paper/newsprint (for removing excess paint from sponges)

Preparation

Clean, fill, sand and seal the surface. Use 2–5 coats of undercoat or gesso on the surface and stipple out any distinct brush-marks. Allow to dry.

POSITIVE SPONGING
Procedure

1. Coat the surface with the background colour using at least two coats. Dry.

2. Wet the sponge and wring it out in a towel, so it is just damp.

3. Dip the sponge lightly into a glaze of the second colour (see page 65) and dab onto butcher's paper to remove excess paint.

4. Holding the sponge lightly with three fingers and the thumb, use a rolling action to move it across the area in clouds of colour, taking it right to the edges. Do not make a pattern of sponge marks. Keep moving the sponge over on itself to create a variety of textures.

Positive and negative sponging, using crimson background and gold sponging. Above left, background for positive sponging; left below, contrasting colour glaze sponged over the background colour. Above right, the same background coated with contrasting colour glaze for negative sponging; below right, background colour revealed as the contrasting glaze is sponged off.

Soften the edges of the sponged colour with a clean area of the sponge.

NEGATIVE SPONGING
Procedure

1. Coat the surface with two coats of the background colour. Dry.

2. Brush on the contrasting colour glaze.

3. While the glaze is still wet, use a damp sponge to remove some of the glaze and reveal the background colour, using the same sponging action described for positive sponging. This results in a stone-like texture.

Stippling, using red background and black stippling. Above, background. Below left, surface stippled with brush-strokes wide apart. Below right, surface stippled with brush-strokes close together.

Stippling

Materials

Sealer: either GMV, gesso, Magic Effects Special Paint or interior undercoat paint

Artist's acrylic colours or interior house paints in two contrasting colours

¾ inch (2 cm) soft brush

Stipple brush

Scumble medium

Butcher's paper/newsprint

Procedure

1. Prepare the background with 2–5 coats of gesso, Magic Effects Special Paint or interior undercoat.

2. Paint on the background colour. Dry.

3. Wipe the stipple brush with the soft brush loaded lightly with the glaze of the second colour.

4. Rub the stipple brush in a circular motion onto butcher's paper to distribute the paint evenly.

5. Pounce the brush up and down on the background colour, perpendicular to the surface of the object being decorated. This action must be done with an even pressure, in drifts, with no straight lines.

Positive dragging

Materials

Sealer: either GMV, gesso, Magic Effects Special Paint or interior house paint

Artist's acrylics or interior house paints in two contrasting colours

Positive dragging, with background colour Cadmium Yellow Medium and dragging in Burnt Sienna. Above, background. Below left, surface dragged in glaze of second colour with vertical brush-strokes. Below right, surface dragged in woven effect with second layer of second-colour brush-strokes at right angles.

Scumble medium

¾ inch (2 cm) firm brush

Butcher's paper/newsprint

Procedure

1. Prepare the surface with 2–5 coats of gesso or undercoat.
2. Paint the surface with the background colour and allow to dry.
3. Load the brush lightly with a glaze of the second colour mixed in the ratio 1:1:1 (see page 65).
4. Pull the loaded brush across the paper to remove any excess paint.
5. Holding the brush at an angle of approximately 45 degrees, pull it across the surface in a series of fine, even pressured, straight vertical lines.

Option For a woven effect, apply straight lines of the second colour, with a lightly loaded brush, at right angles to the first series of lines. This looks especially effective on surfaces where floral images are used, because the background looks like the weave in fabric.

Negative dragging

This background technique is an excellent base for an imitation timber finish, as shown in the photo of the side table on page 63 at the start of this chapter.

Materials

Sealer: either GMV, gesso, Magic Effects Special Paint or interior house paint

Artist's acrylics or interior house paints in two contrasting colours

Scumble medium

¾ inch (2 cm) soft brush

¾ inch (2 cm) flat firm brush

Cotton cloth

Procedure

1. Prepare surface with 2-5 coats of gesso, Magic Effects Special Paint or interior undercoat paint.

Negative dragging, with a Red Oxide background dragged with a Parchment glaze. Above, background. Below left, background painted over with glaze of second colour. Below right, second colour partially removed in negative dragging technique with dry brush.

2. Paint the surface with the background colour and allow to dry.

3. Quickly paint on the glaze of the second colour mixed in the ratio:1:1:1 (see page 65).

4. Pull a dry flat brush through the painted surface in straight vertical lines, wiping the brush onto a cotton cloth after each pass is made.

5. Continue to pull the brush through the paint until the surface is covered with vertical lines.

6. The pressure on the brush will determine and how much paint is taken off the surface. Gentle pressure will give a soft appearance and heavier pressure will give a more defined look to the final effect.

Rag rolling

This technique is excellent on a curved surface where it would be difficult to maintain the straight brush-strokes required for either positive or negative dragging. It is also very effective on a flat surface.

Materials

Sealer: either GMV, gesso, Magic Effects Special Paint or interior house paint, sanded smooth

Artist's acrylic paints in two contrasting colours to suit découpage images (optional top coat: black Japan paint mixed with turpentine at ratio of 5:1 turpentine to black Japan)

Scumble medium

Cotton cloths (upholsterer's cloth or cheesecloth, washed, then dried in a clothes-dryer, leaves crumples in the fabric

Rag rolling, with background of Unbleached Titanium rag rolled with Indian Red Oxide. Above, background. Below left, background painted over with glaze of second colour. Below right, second colour partially removed in rag rolling technique with crumpled cloth.

which make interesting textures when applied to the glazed surface; a folded chamois can be used as an alternative)

Procedure

1. Apply a base colour and allow to dry.

2. Mix a glaze of 1 part artist's acrylic paint to 1 part scumble medium with ½ part water. The glaze colour should contrast with the base colour and tone with the découpage images. (Alternative: glaze of 1 part Black Japan and 5 parts turpentine.)

3. Brush the glaze onto one small area at a time; while it is still wet use the cloth or chamois crumpled in the hand to roll across the surface in random directions. Keep rolling, pressing, dabbing and dragging until the required amount of glaze has been removed to your satisfaction. **Note**: Keep your fingers away from the surface.

4. Keep working over the surface of the object until the entire area has been rag rolled.

The amount of base colour showing through the glaze depends entirely on the pressure used with the cloth to remove the wet glaze.

An example of rag rolling with Black Japan appears on page 64.

Bagging

Materials

Sealer: either GMV, gesso, Magic Effects Special Paint or interior house paint, sanded smooth

Small plastic bag or cling wrap

Artist's acrylic paints—two contrasting colours for single-process, three contrasting colours for double-process

Scumble medium

SINGLE-PROCESS BAGGING
Procedure

1. Apply base colour and allow to dry.

2. Mix a glaze of the other colour, 1 part artist's acrylic paint to 1 part scumble medium with ½ part water, and brush it over the entire surface.

Single-process and double-process bagging, with background colour Black, first glaze Burnt Sienna, second glaze Iridescent Copper. Above left, background. Above right, background painted over with first glaze. Below left, first glaze partially removed with plastic in single-process technique. Below right, second glaze (complete coverage not shown) partially removed in double-process technique.

3. While the glaze is still wet, hold the plastic bag or cling wrap stretched firmly between your hands, pressing it down on the glaze, moving in different directions to create an interesting surface pattern. Allow to dry.

This technique is used on the sides of the box on page 63.

DOUBLE-PROCESS BAGGING
Procedure

Proceed as for single-process bagging, following steps 1, 2 and 3, and allowing to dry.

4. Mix a glaze of the third colour, 1 part artist's acrylic paint to 1 part scumble medium with ½ part water, and brush it over the entire surface. With a clean plastic bag or cling wrap, use the same process to remove the glaze. Some of the base colour and some of the first glaze will show through to create interesting textures and colours.

CHAPTER 5
Special surface effects

Icon effects

Religious icons were often made in the form of a triptych, which is an image in three parts. Folding triptychs, with two hinged wings flanking a central panel, were a popular form of devotional painting in the fifteenth century. The important interior images of the triptych could be protected by closing the wings. The exteriors were painted less colourfully, often with a finish imitating stone or marble, and frames were sometimes gilded, sometimes not.

In this section I have included the techniques of incised

A triptych using the techniques of gilding, antiquing and distressing. The central panel is part of a fifteenth century painting by Stefan Lochner of The Virgin in a Rose Arbour *(1440). This painting, with details in gold, lends itself to elaborate treatment in the form of an icon. The background of the triptych is gilded (see page 79). After the motifs were glued in place, the three panels were antiqued in acrylic with Burnt Umber (see page 32), and the edges distressed where normal wear would occur (see page 91). The central panel and the wings of the triptych are bordered with thick pieces of raised gold paper which match the details in the painting.*

gesso, gilding and the various forms of antiquing which can be used in the creation of an icon. Other special surface effects which can be used include crackling, imitation marble and imitation timber.

General requirements

The first thing is to choose the physical form of the icon—a panel or panels of craftwood, or a wooden mini screen, triptych, plaque, oval, rectangle or some other decorative shape—whose all-over surface must be prepared and sealed appropriately. The next thing is to determine which combination of techniques is appropriate for the images you are planning to use, and to select the appropriate materials.

Artist's acrylic colours to suit images

Brushes in a range of sizes for painting (e.g. # 4 flat, #6 round)

The progressive steps for incising. Rich Gold Powder has been used to gild instead of leaf. Above left, traced cartouche. Above right, incised cartouche. Below left, incised cartouche base-coated with Red Oxide. Below right, Rich Gold Powder applied with incising revealed.

Stylus, nails, small chisel or metal skewer to use for incising

Gold or silver imitation leaf (micro-thin sheets of gold, silver, aluminium or copper)

Soft mop brush for tamping (brushing down) gold leaf

Size

'Bob' for applying size (a very small cotton sack filled with wadding and tied with string or elastic band)

Shellac

Turpentine

Ruler

Sea sponges

Scissors

Cotton gloves

Cotton rags

Black Japan paint

Coloured or clear wax

Rottonstone powder

Antiquing patina (a commercially produced liquid used to give an aged look)

Artist's oil paints in Burnt Umber or Raw Umber (used with antiquing patina)

Artist's acrylic paints in Burnt Umber or Raw Umber (used instead of oil paints and antiquing patina)

Crackle medium

INCISED GESSO

Incising, or cutting a design in layers of gesso, or wood, gives a subtle effect under gilding. Incised areas on early icons and religious paintings served to accentuate the halo, symbol of divinity, which in pre-Christian art had signified the sun's radiance and power. The halo first appeared in Christian art in the fourth century and was a feature of Gothic panel painting, which also often incorporated precious stones. The incised lines attracted light falling onto the painting and distinguished the halo from the sky. Incising designs into a surface can create interest and give another dimension to decorative art pieces.

Don't be constrained by these religious overtones. Incised borders, scrolls and other ornamental patterns (sometimes called cartouches), straight lines, cross-hatching and diamond

Gilding works on flat, raised and incised surfaces The two frames are gilded in variegated leaf. The cherub and finials at the bottom of the picture are gilded with gold powder, the other decorations with gold leaf.

patterns are very effective forms of decoration on many things other than icons.

Materials

Object prepared with up to 10 coats of gesso or Magic Effects Special Paint to provide the necessary thickness for the incising

Carbon paper

Outline of pattern to be incised

Incising tools—stylus (needle-shaped tool), nail or metal skewer

Procedure

1. Using carbon paper under the chosen pattern, trace the outline onto the thickly gessoed surface.

2. With an incising tool, firmly scribe over the carbon outline. The deeper the incising the more effective the finished pattern will be. Try to scribe each section of the outline in one pass.

3. When the incising is complete, apply the background colour and procede with gilding.

GILDING

Gilding is an age-old form of decoration, best suited to small decorative items, or used as embellishment on larger objects such as icons, screens and furniture. It can be also used as a background for the application of pigment, découpage and tortoiseshell.

Master gilders of old had to be thoroughly proficient in various techniques, but for our purposes knowledge of the simple technique called mordant gilding is sufficient. In this technique an adhesive (mordant) is applied to a surface and when it becomes tacky, the leaf is laid over it. Leaf comes in gold, silver, variegated and aluminium. A much cheaper imitation leaf known as Dutch metal is also available in gold and variegated colours. Powders available in Rich Gold, Silver and Copper can also be substituted for leaf. Two advantages of using powder are that there are no visible join lines as there are with leaf, and they are good for uneven or carved surfaces because they easily fill in the indentations.

Attention to preparation of pieces to be gilded is most important since brush-marks, dust and any other imperfection can show through under the gilding. The colour of the base-coat varies with the colour of the leaf used for gilding—use Red Oxide (these days replacing the traditional red clay colour) or Yellow Oxide under gold leaf; blue-grey or black paint under silver and aluminium leaf. Under variegated leaf you can use a colour to suit the predominant colour, for example, Red Oxide for red variegations and Dark Blue for blue variegations.

Materials

Sealer: either GMV, gesso, Magic Effects Special Paint or interior undercoat paint

Acrylic base coat paint to suit the leaf

Acrylic size

Bob applicator

Cotton gloves (to protect the leaf from tarnishing)

Small gold or silver leaf squares (or Dutch metal, Rich Gold, Silver or Copper powder)

Soft mop brush for tamping down gold leaf

Shellac

Brush for application of shellac

GILDING WITH LEAF
Procedure

1. Apply up to five coats of gesso to the prepared surface, sanding and cleaning it to an extremely smooth finish.

2. Apply acrylic paint in the colour to suit the leaf being used (Red or Yellow Oxide for gold leaf; grey-blue or black for aluminium or silver leaf).

3. Dip the bob in the size and wipe any excess liquid onto the side of the container (for a raised or incised surface use a soft brush instead).

4. Apply the size in even strokes, each stroke just overlapping the previous stroke. Try for complete coverage, as the leaf will not adhere to unsized areas.

Steps in the gilding process. Above, undercoat of Red Oxide. Below left, overlapping pieces of gold leaf cover the entire surface. Below right, overlapping pieces of variegated red/gold leaf cover the surface.

A frame gilded in imitation gold leaf (Dutch metal). The four corners of the frame have been incised with an Art Nouveau design (see page 77) to match the style of the painting. The frame has also been distressed by painting on a coat of cupric nitrate, which eats away at the gold until it is neutralised with a water-damp cloth dabbed over the gilded surface. This leaves a green powdery surface on the gilding. These tones of green match the colours in the dress. The découpage, under glass, has a background sponged with green and gold (see page 67) to complement the image. See also découpage under glass on page 51.

5. Wait for about ten minutes or follow the manufacturer's specific instructions for drying time. Test the readiness of the size by touching a knuckle on the surface and lifting off quickly—a 'click' sound indicates the size is ready for the leaf to be applied.

6. Wearing the cotton gloves, cut the leaf into manageable pieces about 2 inches (5 cm) square, all the while holding the leaf between the sheets of rouge paper (the papers separating the sheets of leaf).

7. Position the square of leaf over the sized surface, holding it at the edge and sliding back the rouge paper a little. Gently place the piece of leaf onto the sized surface, sliding the rouge paper further back as the leaf adheres to the surface.

8. Tamp down the leaf with the soft mop brush and continue with the next piece, overlapping each square by about ¼ inch (5 mm).

9. When the surface is completely covered, tamp over the entire surface to flatten the leaf. Remove skewings (surplus pieces of leaf) and continue brushing gently, in a circular motion, to polish the leaf.

10. Seal the gilded surface with one coat of shellac.

11. If using Dutch metal, follow the same procedure.

To gild raised or incised surfaces, prepare the surface as for leaf and paint on an acrylic paint to suit the leaf being used. Apply the size with a lightly loaded soft round brush. When dry, about fifteen minutes (or recommended time), gild using two pieces of leaf, one on top of the other. As the leaf is tamped, the lower piece splits and the upper piece fills the spaces to cover the indented or carved area. Seal with shellac.

GILDING WITH POWDER
Procedure

1. Prepare surface as for gilding with leaf.

2. Paint on Red Oxide acrylic paint for Gold and Copper powder, or Dark Blue for Silver powder.

3. Apply size with a 'bob' to a flat surface or with a brush to indented surfaces. Make sure there is complete coverage.

4. Using a soft round brush, either No 6 or 8, dip into the powder and tap off excess back into container.

5. Gently brush the powder onto the sized surface in even strokes, redipping into powder when necessary.

6. When the entire surface has been brushed with the powder, gently brush off surplus and seal with shellac.

This technique has been used on the copper-gilded cherubs on page 23, and on the gold edge of the table on page 26.

HANDY HINT

Use a dust mask when applying powder and work in a confined space where there is no cross-breeze. Work over plastic to catch excess powder, which can be returned to the container.

Option The finished gilded surface can be painted with a dry ground pigment in a colour to match the images used, mixed with transparent shellac. The glow of the gold shimmers through the pigment and creates a rich surface which can be matched with découpage images. See page 27, where Alizarine Crimson has been mixed with transparent shellac and painted over the gilded surface of the oval box to complement the images on the lid.

ANTIQUING

There are several methods by which you can create an aged, mellowed, 'antique' look—antiquing with patina, either oil or acrylic, with crackle mediums, distressing or using wax.

ANTIQUING WITH PATINA

This effect can be applied to both a finished surface and a surface which has been sealed, but not yet varnished.

If you have used an oil-based antiquing patina before varnishing, the varnish must also be oil-based. If you have used an acrylic paint for antiquing, the antiqued surface must be sealed with GMV before varnishing (with either oil- or water-based varnish).

HANDY HINT

Surfaces with découpage images applied **must** be sealed with GMV before either oil-based antiquing or acrylic antiquing is attempted.

OIL-BASED ANTIQUING
Materials

Antiquing patina

Artist's oil paint (either Burnt Umber, Raw Umber or Burnt Sienna)

Oil-based varnish

Cotton cloth

Procedure

1. Seal the surface with a coat of oil-based varnish. Dry.

2. Wipe over the surface with a thin layer of antiquing patina, using a cloth.

RAW SIENNA

BURNT SIENNA

IRIDESCENT GOLD

RAW UMBER

This board has been antiqued using different coloured paints over a Parchment background. Above left, Raw Sienna. Above right, Burnt Sienna. Below left, Iridescent Gold. Below right, Raw Umber.

3. Using the same cloth, place a dab of the chosen oil colour onto the cloth and rub together to spread the colour. Wipe over areas which are to be toned with the dark colour.

4. Areas which look too dark can be wiped away with the patina on a clean part of the cloth.

5. When thoroughly dry, apply oil-based varnish for the desired finish.

ANTIQUING WITH ACRYLICS
Materials

Artist's acrylic paint (either Burnt Umber, Raw Umber or Burnt Sienna)

Gloss Medium and Varnish (GMV)

Cotton cloth

Varnish

Procedure

1. Seal surface with GMV.

2. Mix a very watery paint of the chosen colour and paint it on the entire surface or on selected areas. Dab with a dry cloth to vary paint distribution.

3. Wipe away paint on areas where antiquing is not required, such as skin or other very light areas. Allow to dry.

4. Seal with GMV before beginning varnishing.

ANTIQUING WITH CRACKLE MEDIUMS
Crackle medium can be applied to small decorative objects, to small sections of an object or to an entire painted surface. Where you have chosen a découpage image of an old oil painting in which cracks have appeared, crackle medium can be used around the image to match the aged look of the painting. Crackle medium can also be used to create interesting textures on the background to the découpage, which can be incorporated into the overall design (see the ostrich egg on page 88, for example).

Crackling can have an oil or acrylic patina wiped over it to accentuate the cracks and add to the aged effect. There are several different ways of using crackle medium, referred to as sandwich crackle, background crackle and surface crackle.

SANDWICH CRACKLE

Crackle medium which is applied between two contrasting colours is referred to as sandwich crackle. It is very important to use paints and mediums which are compatible, for example, use Jo Sonja's Décor Crackle Medium with Jo Sonja's Artist's Gouache.

Materials

Gesso

Artist's acrylics in two contrasting colours

Acrylic crackle medium

Soft brush or sponge brush, about 1 inch (2.5 cm)

Cotton cloth

Varnish

Acrylic paint for antiquing (either Raw Umber, Burnt Sienna or Gold)

Procedure

Always check the manufacturer's instructions for application and drying time. Temperature conditions also play an important part in the success of this technique.

1. Prepare the surface by cleaning, filling, sanding and sealing with gesso or undercoat.

2. Apply two generous coats of the background colour (the first of the two contrasting colours). Allow to dry.

3. Paint crackle medium over the dry background colour using the soft brush or sponge brush. Brush-strokes should be carefully lined up to obtain an overall coverage without skips. Allow to dry.

4. Brush on the second paint colour. Straight lines edge-to-edge (as in the green and blue examples) will give a regular finish. Cross-hatched brush-strokes (as in the red example) will give an irregular effect. A thick coat of paint gives large cracks (as in the blue example). A thin layer of paint results in finer cracks. Take care not to over-brush the paint as this only results in a coagulated mess! If this occurs, wipe off the medium immediately with a damp cloth and reapply.

5. Allow time for the medium to dry and crackling to occur.

6. When thoroughly dry, a patina can be applied by gently

wiping a small amount of artist's acrylic, in either Burnt Umber, Raw Umber or Gold, over the area to be antiqued.

7. Use GMV to seal.

8. The surface can now be finished with varnish.

HANDY HINT

Do not use gold paint **over** the crackle medium as it will not crackle. Gold can be used **under** the crackle medium as the background colour.

BACKGROUND CRACKLE WITH DÉCOUPAGE
Materials

Gesso

Artist's acrylics to match images

Acrylic crackle medium

Soft brush or sponge brush, about 1 inch (2.5 cm)

Cotton cloth

GMV

Wallpaper paste

Varnish

Examples of sandwich crackle. The blue disc shows a thick application of top paint colour in straight lines. The green disc shows a thin application of top paint colour in straight lines. The red disc shows a thin application of top paint colour in cross-hatched strokes.

Acrylic paint in Raw Umber, Burnt Siena or Gold for antiquing (optional)

Procedure

1. Prepare the surface as usual for découpage.
2. Paint on two coats of the background colour and allow to dry.
3. Design the découpage layout by positioning the images on a template. By doing this you can work out where the crackle medium needs to go.
4. Apply the crackle medium, either to the whole piece or to selected areas surrounding the motifs, and allow to dry.
5. Paint on the second contrasting colour carefully, without over-brushing, remembering that the amount of paint you apply will determine the size of the cracks. Allow to dry thoroughly.
6. Seal the surface with two coats of GMV to prevent the crackle medium being reactivated when gluing down the images.

An ostrich egg with crackle in selected areas. The crackle became part of the design for the sky and ice in the skating scene. The background is Dark Blue, the contrasting colour White.

A small vase with crackle applied over the entire piece before the découpage images were glued on. Paint was applied thickly at the top and thinly at the base. The images are taken from the painting Springtime Dance (1909) by the Art Nouveau artist Franz von Stuck. The background colour is Cadmium Yellow, the contrasting colour Ultramarine Blue.

7. Glue down images in the planned design and allow to dry.

8. Seal with two coats of GMV.

9. **Option** After the surface is thoroughly dry, a simple patina can be applied to either the images or the entire area, using artist's acrylic paint in Raw Umber, Burnt Sienna or Gold (or another colour which you may prefer). Thinly spread paint on a cloth and wipe over the areas to be antiqued.

10. Seal the entire surface again with four coats of GMV and proceed with varnishing in the usual manner for découpage.

SURFACE CRACKLE ON DÉCOUPAGE

Crackle medium can also be applied to a finished piece of découpage. This method imitates aged paintings and when antiqued gives a genuine mellowed appearance. I prefer to use Langridge Crackle Varnish, which is applied in a two-part method and is water-based.

A small découpaged box with a fresco background of Parchment, with Naphthol Crimson and Parchment fresco effect (see page 129). The fine cracks were created using Langridge Crackle Varnish. The surface has been antiqued with gold acrylic paint.

Materials

Finished piece of découpage with no wax or liquid polish on the surface

Tack cloth

Langridge Crackle Varnish (two-part)

Soft brushes

Soft cloth

Oil paint in Burnt Umber or Raw Umber, and white spirit, for antiquing (optional)

Procedure

1. Wipe area where crackle medium is to be applied with a tack cloth. Using a soft brush, apply the milky First Coat over the surface. Leave until clear (about thirty minutes).

2. Paint over this with the Top Coat, carefully avoiding any skips, and leave to dry.

3. The cracks will appear after twelve hours, or sooner if working in warm weather. Warming the surface gently with a heater or hair dryer can speed up the procedure.

4. To highlight the craquelure, antique with a 1:1 mix of Burnt Umber (or Raw Umber) oil paint and white spirit

painted over the surface. When touch-dry, wipe surface with a soft cloth to reveal the colour in the cracks. Seal with oil-based varnish.

DISTRESSING

This type of antiquing is done before the découpage process, after the base colours have been applied to the surface. The areas to be distressed are those which would naturally attract most wear from use.

Materials

Base colour to suit découpage images

220 garnet paper (or 400 wet-and-dry sandpaper, or #0000 steel wool)

Sanding block (cork or rubber)

Examples of distressing. Above left, painted background of Parchment with a top coat of Naphthol Crimson and Parchment. Above right, distressing with garnet paper. Below left, distressing with wet-and-dry sandpaper (used dry). Below right, distressing with #0000 steel wool.

Procedure

1. Apply two or three coats of a base colour to suit the découpage images.

2. You can distress the required areas using any one of three methods:

   A. With garnet paper over a sanding block, work in a circular motion with medium pressure to rub off some of the base colour in some areas.

   B. With wet-and-dry sandpaper used dry, place the paper on a sanding block and work in a vertical direction with a medium to hard pressure in selected areas or where natural wear would occur.

   C. Work the #0000 steel wool in a circular motion on areas where most wear would occur naturally.

WAX ANTIQUING

Wax antiquing takes place as a final polish, or after the completion of varnishing. The wax is applied over the entire surface and then rubbed off in areas which are lighter, such as skin tones or the pale highlights featured in the cut-out motifs.

Materials

Clear wax

Rottonstone powder

Soft cloth

Procedure

1. Blend a small amount of wax and rottonstone powder to a creamy mixture (about 1 tablespoon of wax to ¼ teaspoon of powder). Use more powder for a darker colour.

2. Using a cloth dipped in the creamy mixture, apply to selected areas or all over the surface.

3. This mixture can also be used on crackled areas of work to accentuate the crackled effect.

Oriental finishes

ORIENTAL BACKGROUND COLOURS

The background colours used on high-gloss Japanese lacquerware, which was one of the original sources of inspiration for découpage, were traditionally red and black. In more recent times, dark green and a rather mustardy yellow have also been used.

This finish is suitable for ornaments, plates and boxes.

Materials

Artist's acrylic colours

Traditional
Base colour—Black
Surface colour—Cadmium Red Medium Hue/Lacquer Red, Scarlet Red or Napthol Red Light

Modern
Base colour—Hookers Green Dark
Surface colour—one part Yellow Oxide to one part Cadmium Yellow Medium

GMV

Stipple brush

Sea sponge

Bristle brushes

Toothbrush

Burnt Umber artist's acrylic

Scumble medium

Paper towels

400 wet-and-dry sandpaper or #0000 steel wool

Procedure

1. Prepare the surface by filling, sanding and sealing.
2. Paint on three coats of artists' acrylic Black paint. Sand smooth between coats.
3. Seal with GMV.
4. Paint on one coat of your chosen red.
5. Gently sand smooth.
6. Apply a second smooth coat of watery red, trying to minimise brush marks.
7. Distress the area using either the wet-and-dry sandpaper (used dry) or the steel wool, working with a circular motion. Allow the black to show through where natural wear would occur.

8. Using a toothbrush dipped into a watery mix of ½ part Black to 1 part Burnt Umber, spatter generously to give an aged appearance. Dry.

9. Mix a glaze of 1 part red, 1 part Burnt Umber, 2 parts scumble medium and 3 parts water and stipple unevenly over the piece. Leave to dry.

10. Gently rub the surface with #0000 steel wool until smooth.

11. If you are gilding any part of the project, do so at this point.

12. Seal with GMV.

13. Finish with high-gloss varnish.

The same procedure is followed for the green and yellow finish. At step 9, however, the proportions for the glaze mix are different—⅓ part each of White, Cadmium Yellow

Process for Oriental background colours of red and black. Above left, black background. Above right, the red painted over black. Below left, red after distressing. Below right, spattering and stippling completed.

*Ginger jar finished in
Oriental background colours
of green and yellow.*

Medium and Yellow Oxide, 1 part Burnt Umber, 2 parts scumble medium and 3 parts water.

ORIENTAL TIMBER FINISH

This painted finish imitates the bark used in Japan for small boxes and decorative objects.

Materials

Artist's acrylic colours:
    White
    Cadmium Yellow Medium
    Yellow Oxide
    Red Oxide
    Burnt Sienna
    Cobalt Blue
    Burnt Umber
    Black

Black Japan mixed with turpentine 1:4 (optional)

GMV

Scumble medium

Oil-based varnish

Paper towels

A tray featuring the Oriental timber finish, demonstrating the result of applying Rich Gold Powder over the black glaze and varnish. It is découpaged in a Japanese theme with cranes. The water features are gilded using Rich Gold Powder (see page 79).

Sharp stick, stylus, wooden or metal skewer

Bristle brush

Palette knife or plastic knife

600 wet-and-dry sandpaper

Sponge brushes

Sea sponges

Rich Gold Bronzing Powder

Nylon stocking-covered open-ended cylinder for dusting gold powder

Dust mask

Procedure

1. Prepare the surface by filling, sanding and sealing.

2. Paint on three to five coats of the base colour mixture— 1 part White, ¼ part Yellow Oxide and ¼ part Cadmium Yellow Medium. Sand smooth after each coat.

3. Seal with two coats of GMV and varnish.

4. Mix a dark brown glaze—1 part Red Oxide, 5 parts Burnt Sienna, 2 parts Cobalt Blue, 2 parts scumble and 2 parts

water. This should be applied in one thick, smooth coat. Use the sea sponge and sponge brush to achieve coverage with no brush-marks. Allow to dry.

5. Using 600 wet-and-dry sandpaper (use dry), gently sand in a circular motion to ensure a smooth surface.

6. Using the stick, skewer or stylus, etch off some dark brown glaze in small irregular strips on about 10% of the area to reveal the yellow beneath. If necessary, use water with the tool to help remove the paint.

7. After the object is completely dry, apply a glaze of 1 part Black, 1 part Burnt Umber and 1 part water. Allow to dry. Alternatively, paint on a coat of Black Japan mixed with turps 1:4 and allow to dry.

8. Coat the surface with oil-based gloss varnish and allow to set for about two minutes.

Steps in creating the Oriental timber finish. Above left, base colour. Above right, brown glaze applied. Below left, some of the glaze etched off with stylus. Below right, black glaze has been applied and Rich Gold Bronzing Powder scattered over varnished surface.

9. Dust the surface with Rich Gold Bronzing Powder. Gently blow the powder through a piece of nylon fabric stretched over an open-ended cylinder so a fine veil of gold scatters over the surface.

10. Dry overnight and finish with two coats of oil-based gloss varnish.

Marble illusions

Have you ever travelled to the northern Italian town of Cararra? Tons of marble, of every imaginable colour, lie awaiting transportation in holding yards which can be seen from the road.

The beauty of marble has been appreciated for centuries. Although the real thing is beyond the reach of most, faux marble surfaces are relatively easy to create. The white, cream, black, green, black and gold, and red marble finishes described here can be adapted to suit your découpage design and can even be combined in an inlay effect.

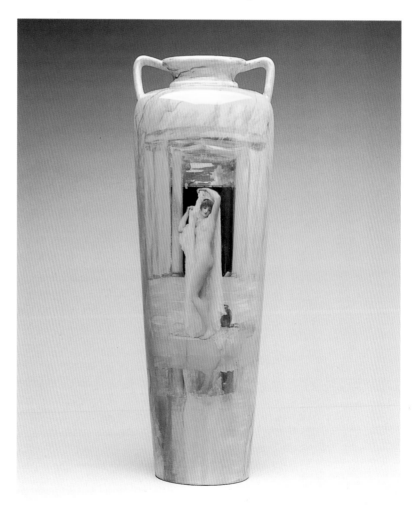

Ceramic urn with white-grey marble background featuring a découpage image from The Bath of Psyche *(1890) by Lord Leighton. The technique for white-grey marble is the same as for cream marble (see page 100).*

WHITE MARBLE
Materials

Sealer: either GMV, gesso, Magic Effects Special Paint or interior undercoat paint

White artist's acrylics or interior house paint

Water-soluble pastels:
Black
Grey
Brown
Yellow Oxide

Soft round or flat brush (No 4 or 6)

Sea sponge

Palette

Non-yellowing varnish

The simple process of creating white marble using water-soluble pastels. Above left, white background. Above right, veins drawn in with pastels. Below left, watery White paint applied to some pastel veins. Below right, completed marble effect with pastels and watery White spread over surface.

Procedure

1. Prepare the surface by cleaning, filling, sanding and sealing.

2. Paint on two coats of white as the background. Sand smooth so no brush marks show. Dry.

3. Using all four soluble pastels, draw veins (branching wobbly lines, see example) over the surface in selected places.

4. On a palette, make a watery mix of white acrylic paint.

5. Using the round or flat brush loaded with watery white, paint alongside the soluble pastel veins, on both sides, one colour at a time, bleeding some of the colour into the watery mix to spread the colour over the white background. Wash the brush between colours. Throughout this process, use the sea sponge to dab off some of the paint to break the vein lines and vary the colour density.

6. Varnish with a high-gloss non-yellowing varnish.

CREAM MARBLE
Materials

Sealer: either GMV, gesso, Magic Effects Special Paint or interior house paint

Artist's acrylic paints:
    White
    Cream
    Yellow Ochre
    Burnt Sienna
    Iridescent Gold (optional)

Scumble medium and water

1 inch (2.5 cm) flat brush

Sea sponges

#000 liner brush, or feather

Cloth or paper towel

Procedure

1. Paint the surface with two coats of white acrylic paint. Allow to dry.

2. Paint the surface with a cream glaze of 2 parts White, 1 part

Yellow Ochre, 1 part scumble medium and 1 part water.

3. Using a damp sea sponge lift off about 5% of the cream glaze.

4. Mix a glaze of 1 part scumble, 1 part water and 1 part Burnt Sienna and apply with a sea sponge over the cream. Quickly lift off 50% of this wet glaze with a clean damp sea sponge, taking care to soften the edges of the sponging.

5. Using the same glaze, apply veins using the liner brush or feather. Use the feather first on the tip, then on the flat width. Break or shatter the veining by sponging over the line of the vein with a clean damp sponge.

6. Remove colour from between a few pairs of veins, using a rag or paper towel. Dry.

7. Mix a glaze of 1 part scumble medium, 1 part water and 1 part Cream and apply to 95% of the surface, using the sea sponge.

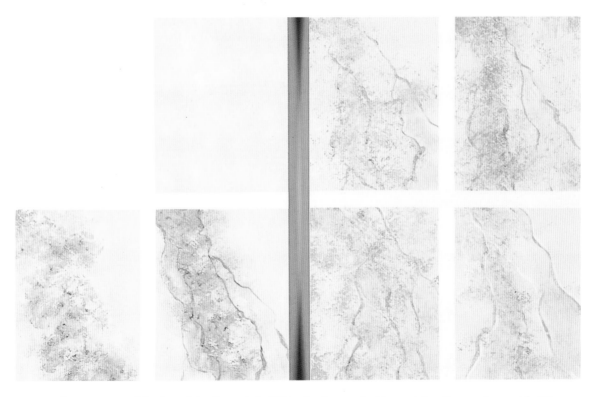

Process for cream marble. Board 1: Above left, White background. Above right, Cream glaze with 5% lifted off. Below left, Burnt Sienna sponged over Cream. Below right, Burnt Sienna veins applied. Board 2: Above left, colour removed between veins with Cream glaze sponged over. Above right, Gold sponging applied. Below left, White veins added. Below right, completed cream marble (without optional Gold sponging).

This trunk, découpaged with the story of the Twelve Dancing Princesses, has a surface of cream marble finished with Iridescent Gold to match the fairytale theme. The carved corners and decorative pieces, glued in place after the final polish, have been gilded with variegated gold leaf. The tassel on the handle is made of silk and embroidered with silk ribbon roses. The interior of the trunk is lined with dark green velvet. A posy of pale pink roses in one corner conceals a light-sensitive music box.

8. Apply a few white veins with a liner brush to highlight the Burnt Sienna veins.

Option Give a fantasy glow to the marble by sponging on watery Iridescent Gold to about 5% of the surface.

BLACK MARBLE
Materials

Sealer: either GMV, gesso, Magic Effects Special Paint or interior house paint

Artists' acrylic paints (or interior acrylic house paint) in Black and White

Scumble medium

Soft flat paint brush, about 5 cm (2 inches)

No 4 round brush

000 liner brush

Stipple brush

Sea sponge

Feather

Butcher's paper/newsprint

Cotton cloth

Procedure

1. Prepare and seal the surface by cleaning, filling, sanding and undercoating.
2. Paint on two base coats of Black acrylic paint.
3. Stipple to eliminate brush-marks and allow to dry.
4. Make a watery glaze of White acrylic paint.
5. Dip damp sea sponge into white glaze, squeeze out excess and dab sponge onto the paper.

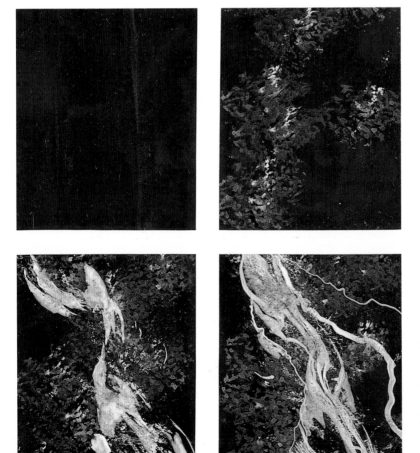

Simple process for black marble. Above left, Black background. Above right, White sponging applied. Below left, White feathered vein. Below right, White veins added with # 4 brush and 000 liner.

6. Apply sponge to surface in clouds of colour and dab with a damp cloth to blur.

7. Using a thicker glaze of White, draw a feather through the mix and remove excess paint on the paper.

8. Pull the feather on the edge, and then on the flat, down across the entire surface to make a large fluttery vein.

9. Dab the vein with a clean damp sponge to break the line.

10. Using the same White paint mix, and a No 4 round brush, pull and roll the brush to create a few veins originating from the larger feathered one. Dab with a damp sea sponge to break the vein line.

11. Load a 000 liner brush with a very watery glaze of White paint and pull some tiny fine veins through the marble.

12. When thoroughly dry, protect the marble surface with a non-yellowing varnish.

GREEN MARBLE
Materials

Sealer: either GMV, gesso, Magic Effects Special Paint or interior house paint

Artist's acrylic paints (or interior house paints):
    White
    Hookers Green Deep Hue
    Black
    Unbleached Titanium
    Chromium Oxide Green
    Ultramarine Blue
    Burnt Umber
    Alizarin Crimson
    Raw Sienna

Soft # 6 flat paint brush

4 round brush

000 liner brush

Stipple brush

2 inch (5 cm) soft brush

Sea sponge

Feather

Toothbrush

Cotton cloth

Procedure

1. Prepare and seal the surface by cleaning, filling, sanding and undercoating.

2. Paint on two coats of the base colour of Hookers Green Deep Hue and stipple to remove brush marks. Dry thoroughly.

3. Paint on marble veins using the #6 flat brush (or a feather on the flat), using a watery glaze of 1 part Unbleached Titanium, 1 part Chromium Oxide Green and ½ part Ultramarine Blue. Roll a damp sea sponge over the veins to blur them and carry the colour across the entire surface, shading with the paint on the sponge.

4. Mix three glazes following the procedure on page 65:
   Glaze 1: 1 part Hookers Green, ¼ part Black
   Glaze 2: 1 part Hookers Green, 1 part Burnt Umber, ¼ part Ultramarine Blue
   Glaze 3: White

   Using the No 4 brush, paint on a few veins using each of the three glazes in selected areas. The action with the brush involves pulling, twisting and turning the brush

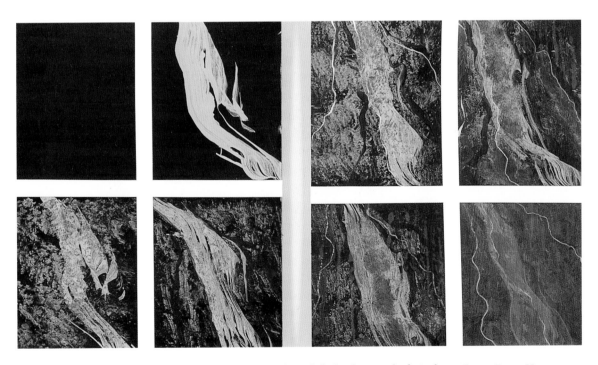

Step-by-step process for green marble. Board 1: Above left, background of Hookers Green Deep Hue. Above right, vein painted in using feather. Below left, sponging over vein. Below right, veins of glazes 1 and 2. Board 2: Above left, white veins added. Above right, wiped out areas between veins. Below left, glazes 4 and 5 applied. Below right, completed green marble.

alongside the original large veins, overlapping in some places and branching off in others. After each vein has been applied, use a damp sponge to wipe out small areas of paint between some veins and dab with a dry cloth to blur the area. This gives an illusion of greater depth.

5. Mix three more glazes:

   Glaze 4: 1 part Ultramarine Blue, ½ part Raw Sienna

   Glaze 5: 1 part Chromium Oxide Green, ¼ part Black, 1 part Ultramarine Blue

   Glaze 6: 1 part Alizarine Crimson, ¼ part Black

   Note Each of these glaze mixes is now watered down—1 part glaze to 4 parts water. Using the flat soft brush, paint each of these very watery glazes over the entire surface and sponge off in selected areas to give different colour tones. Allow each glaze to dry before proceeding to the next one.

6. Spatter a little of glazes 4 and 5 in selected areas, using the toothbrush.

7. Make a white glaze mixed to a creamy consistency (1 part white, 2 parts water) and use the 000 liner brush to paint in a few more fine veins and highlight one side of some of the veins of the other colours.

8. Protect the marble with a coat of non-yellowing varnish.

A lamp base using this method of marbling is seen on page 20.

INLAY

Marble lends itself to tiled and inlay effects. A combination of different marbles makes it easy to achieve a uniquely interesting object. Using the procedures in this chapter, faux tiles or inlays of various marbles can be applied to many different objects. Simple straight-edged designs like squares and hexagons are most successful. Colours which look good together for inlaid marble include black and white, and green and cream.

Procedure

1. After preparing and sealing the surface in the usual way, measure the area for the contrasting marble and mask off with tape. Use a simple straight-edged design like squares or hexagons.

2. Apply the first marble colour over the inlay area. When it is dry, protect it with fresh tape.

A marble inlay box. The outer part of the lid was painted first in cream marble (see page 100), then masked while the inner 'inlaid' section was worked in green marble (page 104). A fine black line of 'grouting' separates the inlay.

3. Proceed with the second marble colour on the unmarbled area, crossing over onto the masking tape. When dry, gently lift off the masking tape. Add more veins and highlights if necessary.

4. The joins between the two marble colours can be accented by making a straight line of either grey or black to imitate a grouting line.

Finish the piece in gloss varnish.

Process for marble inlay using black and white marbles. Above, area masked off for black marble in the centre of the rectangle. Below, central area of black masked off while white marble surround is being painted.

BLACK AND GOLD MARBLE

This beautiful marble finish is suitable for decorating ornaments, boxes and small objects and makes a wonderful fantasy finish for larger columns and tabletops. The effect is of a misty black background with a gold chain veining through.

Materials

Artist's acrylic colours (or interior house paints in similar colours for large areas):
    Black
    White (or Iridescent White)
    Iridescent Gold
    Yellow Oxide
    Burnt Sienna

Scumble medium

Sea sponges

Feather

Liner brush (about 000)

No 4 (approx.) soft brush

Preparation

Prepare the surface by cleaning, filling, sanding and sealing. Coat with two to four coats of gesso, sanding smooth between coats. Base-coat over the gesso with two coats of Black, sanding smooth between coats.

Procedure

1. Mix a watery wash of white. (Iridescent white is particularly effective.) Using a sea sponge, daub cloudy

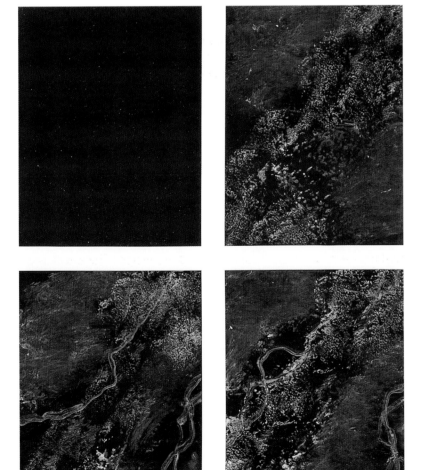

The process for black and gold marble. Above left, Black background. Above right, Iridescent White sponging. Below left, veins of gold making a chain.. Below right, completed marble with Yellow Oxide and Burnt Sienna veins.

A box featuring black and gold marble background behind a 1926 Erté theatrical design, Angel Harpist Costume, Design for The Blues, George White's Scandal. *Edge of box gilded using Rich Gold Powder (see page 82).*

mists of the wash across the object, covering about a quarter of the surface area.

2. On a palette, mix a glaze of 1 part Iridescent Gold, 1 part scumble medium and ½ part water. Using a liner brush loaded with the glaze, draw in a vein, twisting the brush from side to side and letting it flop down onto the surface from time to time.

3. Draw in a second vein, crossing over the first, to make a chain. Press a damp sea sponge across the veins to break the chain.

4. On a palette mix a glaze of 1 part Yellow Oxide, 1 part scumble medium and ½ part water. Load the liner brush with the glaze and draw on a vein, following one of the gold veins to highlight the gold and throw a shadow behind it. (Burnt Sienna or Burnt Orange could be used as well, or instead.)

5. Use a high-gloss varnish to finish the marble.

RED MARBLE
Materials

Sealer: either GMV, gesso, Magic Effects Special Paint or interior house paint

Artist's acrylics or interior house paint:
    White
    Cadmium Red Medium Hue
    Red Oxide
    Burnt Sienna
    Naphthol Red Light
    Vivid Red Orange

Burnt Umber
Raw Umber
Ultramarine Blue

Scumble medium

2 inch (5 cm) soft flat brush

No 4 round

000 liner

Stipple brush

Sea sponge

Feather

Brown paper folded on the diagonal to make a fan-type fold

Plastic wrap

High-gloss non-yellowing varnish

The process for red marble. Board 1: Above left, White background. Above right, red glaze over white. Below left, pouncing with folded paper. Below right, glaze of Red Oxide, Burnt Sienna, Naphthol Red Light and Vivid Red Orange dabbed with plastic wrap. Board 2: Above left, white feathered vein. Above right, smaller veins added. Below left, sponging with Burnt Umber and Ultramarine Blue mix. Below right, grey glaze and outlined grey shapes.

Procedure

1. Prepare the surface by cleaning, filling, sanding and sealing.

2. Paint on two coats of White for the base colour and dry.

3. Paint on a glaze of 2 parts Cadmium Red Medium Hue, 1 part Red Oxide.

4. Pounce the folded brown paper across the wet glaze to create veins on the surface.

5. Allow to partially dry.

6. Paint on a glaze of equal parts of Red Oxide, Burnt Sienna, Naphthol Red Light and Vivid Red Orange. Experiment with the ratio of colours to get a redder or more orange colour if preferred. Dab with plastic wrap while wet.

7. Mix a watery White paint mix and use a feather pulled through it to draw a few large veins across the surface. Sponge across veins to break up the colour.

8. From each of the large veins draw a few smaller veins using the No 4 round brush and the White paint mix.

9. Using the 000 brush draw some tiny white veins from the small veins. Allow to dry.

10. Sponge the red areas with a watery mixture of equal parts Burnt Umber and Ultramarine Blue.

11. Sponge over the entire area with a glaze of light grey obtained by mixing 3 parts White, 1 part Ultramarine Blue and 1 part Raw Umber.

12. Add more White to the grey glaze and outline some of the grey shapes with the 000 liner brush.

13. Protect the marble with a coat of high-gloss varnish.

Stone finishes

SANDSTONE

This background gives the impression of a surface of stone bricks and is particularly effective on larger areas. It is, however, essential to work on only a small area at a time, breaking large areas up into sections.

Materials

Sealer: either GMV, gesso, Magic Effects Special Paint or interior house paint

Artist's' acrylics:
  Yellow Orange Azo
  White
  Grey
  Background: 1 part Yellow Orange Azo + 3 parts White
  Glaze 1: 1 part Yellow Orange Azo + 5 parts White
  Glaze 2: 1 part Yellow Orange Azo + 7 parts White
  Glaze 3: ½ part Grey + 1 part Glaze 1

Scumble medium

¾ inch (2 cm) soft brush

Feather

Chamois or plastic

Procedure for sandstone. Above left, background. Above right, diagonals of Glaze 1 added. Below left, diagonals of Glaze 2 added. Below right, finished sandstone with Glaze 3 added and chamois and feather work completed.

Procedure

1. Prepare the area with 2 to 5 coats of gesso, Magic Effects Special Paint or interior undercoat paint.

2. Paint on background colour mix and allow to dry.

3. Paint on Glaze 1 with a soft brush, making irregular diagonal lines about 1¼ inches (3 cm) wide.

4. While Glaze 1 is still wet, repeat with Glaze 2 and Glaze 3 to make more diagonal lines.

5. Press the crumpled chamois or plastic very lightly onto the still-wet glazed surface. Refold and press again, continuing across the surface to create a stone pattern.

6. Hold the feather on the diagonal and comb across the wet glaze using the tips of the feather.

Option The sandstone can later be sectioned off into blocks by painting in shadow lines to imitate mortar joints.

GRANITE

Granite is found in a great variety of colours which makes the technique very useful as a background. Colours can vary from rich earthy tones to grey, a deep blue tone, pinks and white. This technique is based on using three values of a particular colour to the create the effect. Indian Red Oxide as the initial colour for pink granite, for example, is mixed with various amounts of White to create the three values required to produce the granite effect. The granite on the sample board is worked in pink tones, the découpaged box in earth-tones (mostly orange).

Materials

Sealer: either GMV, gesso, Magic Effects Special Paint or interior house paint

Artist's acrylics:

Pink granite
Indian Red Oxide
White
Black
Iridescent White
Interference Red

Earth-toned granite
Scarlet Red
Cadmium Red Light Hue

White
Black
Iridescent White
Interference Red

Blue granite
Phthalocyanine Blue
White
Black
Dark Grey
Iridescent White
Interference Blue

White granite
White
Black
½ part Payne's Grey + 1 part White
Iridescent White

Grey granite
Payne's Grey
Ivory

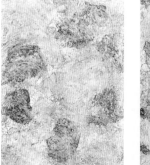
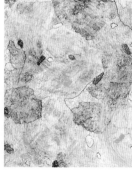

Left: The granite process (pink granite). Above left, white background. Above right, three values of Indian Red Oxide brushed on. Below left, the effect after sponging completed. Below right, quartz 'crystals' outlined in black, with the addition of a few cracks.

Right: Powder box with orange and grey granite background to Caravaggio's The Lute Player *(1595).*

Black
Phthalocyanine Blue
Iridescent White
Interference Blue

Scumble medium

¾ inch (2 cm) soft brush

No 6 flat brush

Sea sponges of various size openings and textures

PINK GRANITE
Procedure

1. Prepare the surface with 2 to 5 coats of gesso, Magic Effects Special Paint or interior housepaint.

2. Paint the entire surface with White acrylic paint and dry thoroughly.

3. Mix glazes of the dark, medium and light values required by using Indian Red Oxide as value one, Indian Red Oxide mixed with White as value two and Indian Red Oxide mixed with more White as value three. Apply patches of each colour to the surface in cross-hatched brush-strokes. If working on a large area do small sections at a time.

4. Using slightly damp sea sponges, work over the glazed area in a pouncing/dabbing/rolling/swirling action to lift off the glaze and reveal the white background, as shown on the sample board. Keep using a clean part of the sponge and changing the size of the sponges to give a variety of textures. The desired outcome is a mottled effect with swirls and intermingling of colours, with the white background showing through.

5. Keep working on small areas at a time until the entire surface has been covered with the granite effect.

6. Using the small flat brush, paint in a few small solid blocks of the darkest value. Allow to dry thoroughly.

7. Using the Iridescent White, paint over some very small white areas to make 'quartz crystal' highlights. Outline these in black with a liner brush. Paint a few tiny darker areas with Interference Red and outline. Add a few 'cracks' with the liner brush. Allow to dry thoroughly.

8. Finish with a water-based gloss varnish.

Follow the same basic process to make granite in the other colours. There is plenty of scope for experimentation-you might like to make up a sample board of your own with the 'recipe' for each effect noted alongside.

LAPIS LAZULI
Materials

Sealer: either GMV, gesso, Magic Effects Special Paint or interior house paint

Artist's acrylics:
  Ultramarine Blue
  Black
  White
  Iridescent Bronze

Sea sponge

Nos 3 and 6 flat or round brushes

Liner brush or feather

½ inch (12 mm) flat brush

Scumble medium

Toothbrush

The process for lapis lazuli. Board 1: Above left, White base coat with Iridescent Bronze sponged on. Above right, dark blue glaze over. Below left, dark blue glaze sponged off and grey vein added. Below right, feathered vein added. Board 2: Above left, watery translucent blue glaze painted over. Above right, Iridescent Bronze veins added. Below left, Iridescent Bronze spattered. Below right, finished lapis lazuli.

A cutlery box with lapis lazuli background and featuring a pastoral scene by François Boucher (1703–1770). Gold cartouches were used to embellish this Rococo painting and so complement the artwork's decorative style.

Procedure

1. Prepare the surface by cleaning, filling, sanding and sealing. Coat with 2 to 4 coats of gesso, sanding smooth between coats.

2. Base-coat with White and allow to dry.

3. Lightly sponge Iridescent Bronze over about 5% of the area. Dry.

4. Brush on a glaze of blue. For a deep blue use 1 part Ultramarine Blue to 1 part Black. For a lighter lapis blue use 3 parts Ultramarine Blue to 1 part black, using equal parts of paint, scumble and water for the glaze.

5. Stipple with a damp sponge to open up the paint to reveal the white base colour, as for the granite process on page 114.

6. Brush on veins of watery grey, to about 10% of the area. Touch lightly with a sponge to lift off some colour. Allow to dry.

7. Dip liner brush or feather in watery white and pull through parts of the surface to create veins. Break the vein lines with the sea sponge. Allow to dry.

8. Paint over the surface with a watery translucent glaze of 1 part Ultramarine Blue, 1 part Black, 1 part scumble medium and 3 to 4 parts water.

9. **Option** In small areas paint short wide irregular veins of Iridescent Bronze with the No 3 round brush.

10. Using the toothbrush, spatter Iridescent Bronze over some areas.

11. Varnish with a non-yellowing varnish.

MALACHITE
Materials

Sealer: either gesso or acrylic paint

Artist's acrylic paints:

Base coat
> Turquoise Green (or Phthalocyanine Green and Titanium White, mixed 2:1)
> Hookers Green Deep Hue
> Black

Scumble medium

½ inch (12 mm) flat brush

'Wipe-out' tools, roughly torn cardboard pieces about 1½ x 1¼ inch (4 x 3 cm)

Toothbrush

Procedure

1. Prepare surface by sealing, sanding and undercoating with 3 to 5 coats of gesso or acrylic paint and sanding smooth.

2. Base-coat with Turquoise Green and allow to dry.

3. Mix a glaze of 1 part Hookers Green Deep Hue, 1 part scumble medium and ½ part water. Fully load the brush with the glaze and paint onto a small section of a large area (or the whole surface of a smaller object). Stipple out any brush-marks. If the area is large, you can create a tiled or inlaid effect by masking off and working in smaller sections.

4. Using the cardboard wipe-out tools, gently draw fan or semi-circular shapes in the wet glaze by pivoting the

cardboard, one end held in place while the other end makes the pattern. Try to achieve a 'wobble' in the shape for a more authentic look. Wipe the glaze from the cardboard after each pattern is made.

5. Continue working semi-circles or fans next to and overlapping each other until the entire surface is patterned. Keep changing the wipe-out tool to get a variety of sizes. Corrections can be made by painting over unsatisfactory patterns with more glaze and working new patterns.

6. Dip the toothbrush into some of the watered-down glaze to which has been added a very small amount of Black (just enough to make a contrast with the original). Spatter lightly over the entire object.

7. Dry thoroughly.

8. Finish with a gloss varnish.

Malachite process. Above left, base coat. Above right, glaze coat applied. Below left, first working with wipe-out tools. Below right, wipe-out pattern refined and spattered with watered-down glaze.

Malachite vase with an illuminated motif (the background for the image has been gilded). Image taken from The Village Fair *by Adolf Schroedter (1805–1875).*

Tortoiseshell patterns

OIL TORTOISESHELL

Tortoiseshell is useful as a finish on small areas of larger objects, or for small decorative items. The tortoiseshell finish looks particularly beautiful painted over a gilded surface. Alternatively, it can be worked on a golden-yellow painted surface. Using various proportions of the three colours required for the process will give quite different results.

Materials

Materials for gilding, as listed on page 79 (or Yellow Oxide artist's acrylic base with Iridescent Gold painted over)

1:1 mix of scumble and white spirit

½ inch (12 mm) firm brush

Soft mop brush

Black Japan paint (or a creamy mixture of Burnt Umber and
Black artist's oils)

Artist's oils:
Burnt Sienna
Burnt Umber
Black

Plastic wrap or newspaper

Toothbrush

Sea sponge

Isocol (or white spirit or turpentine)

Oil-based varnish

Procedure

1. Prepare and seal the surface.
2. Gild the surface, following the instructions on page 80.

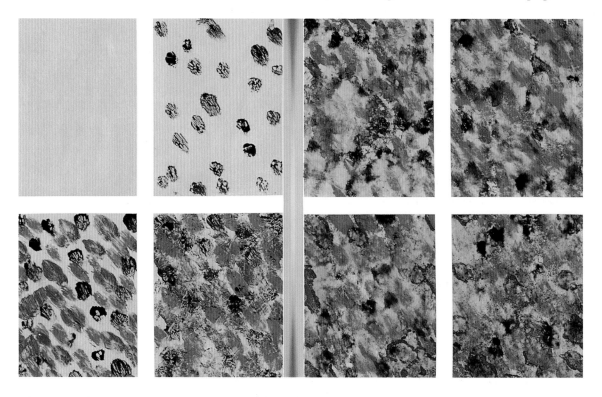

The process for oil tortoiseshell with painted background. Board 1: Above left, Iridescent Gold over Yellow Oxide. Above right, Black Japan brush-strokes. Below left, Burnt Sienna and Burnt Umber strokes added. Below right, crumpled plastic has blended the colours. Board 2: Above left, turpentine sponged onto paint. Above right, mop brush applied diagonally. Below left, Black paint outlines added. Below right, finished tortoiseshell with spatter of Black.

This box is finished in oil tortoiseshell over a gilded surface. The découpaged painting on the lid, by Anne-Louis Girodet de Roucy-Trioson Montargis, is titled The Sleep of Endymion *(1793).*

(Alternatively, paint on a base-coat of 1 coat of Yellow Oxide with 2 coats of Iridescent Gold over it.)

3. Coat the surface generously with the scumble and white spirit mix to allow the paint colours to run smoothly into each other.

4. Using the Black Japan paint (or the creamy mixture of Black and Burnt Umber), brush colour diagonally across the object in small random strokes. Alternate this with Burnt Sienna and Burnt Umber, painting in the same direction. The colours should drift over the surface in a tortoiseshell-like pattern. Leave space between the colours so the glow of the gold base colour shows through.

5. Crumple some plastic or newspaper and dab over the surface to blend the colours. Using a sea sponge dipped in turpentine, dab over the entire surface to soften the effect and blend the colours.

6. Use the tip of the mop brush to feather across the surface diagonally, to blend and soften the paint into a naturalistic pattern.

7. **Option** Brush on touches of Black artist's oil in uneven oval shapes. Spatter the surface with a toothbrush dipped in Black artist's oil mixed with a drop of turpentine.

8. When the surface is thoroughly dry, apply a high gloss oil-based varnish to protect the surface.

TORTOISESHELL LACE

This extremely simple oil-based finish gives an interesting background for découpage.

Tortoiseshell lace process over painted background. Above left, Red Oxide background. Above right, Iridescent Gold. Below left, Black Japan painted over gold surface. Below right, gold background showing through after surface sprayed with one burst of Isocol.

Small tortoiseshell lace boxes découpaged with paintings by Gerrit Van Honthorst—The Guitar Player and The Cellist *(1631).*

Materials

Materials for gilding, as listed on page 79 (or artist's acrylics in Red Oxide and Iridescent Gold)

Black Japan paint

Turpentine

Isocol

Oil-based varnish

Procedure

1. Prepare the surface for gilding.

2. Gild the surface (or paint with 2 coats of Iridescent Gold over Red Oxide and allow to dry).

3. Paint over the piece with Black Japan thinned with turpentine (about 1 part Black Japan to 5 parts turpentine).

4. While paint is still wet, spray Isocol or turpentine over the entire surface. About four or five sprays should disperse enough paint to reveal an attractive pattern of the gold background.

5. Allow to dry thoroughly.

6. Varnish with oil-based varnish to a high gloss finish.

ACRYLIC TORTOISESHELL
Materials

Base-coat: Yellow Oxide artist's acrylic or Jennifer Bennell's Gold Wall Finish

Artist's acrylics:
Iridescent Gold
Acra Gold
Black
Burnt Umber

Scumble medium

½ inch (12 mm) firm flat brush

Soft mop brush

Plastic wrap

Sea sponge

The process for acrylic tortoiseshell. Above left, base-coat of Jennifer Bennell's Gold Wall Finish. Above right, diagonal strokes of Acra Gold, Iridescent Gold and circles of Burnt Umber. Below left, crumpled plastic and water sponging to disperse paint. Below right, mop brush has been used on the diagonal; irregular shapes painted and Black spattered on.

Toothbrush

Water-based varnish

Procedure

1. Prepare surface by sealing, sanding and undercoating. Base-coat with Yellow Oxide or Jennifer Bennell's Gold Wall Finish, and sand smooth.

2. Paint prepared surface with Iridescent Gold in short firm diagonal strokes. Allow to dry.

3. Paint Scumble medium over the surface.

4. Brush Acra Gold in short firm diagonal strokes, all in the one direction, over about 40% of the area.

5. Apply Burnt Umber and Black in separate small, uneven circular patterns to about 60% of the area, overlapping the Acra Gold in places.

6. Crumple plastic wrap and dab over the surface; follow up with a damp sea sponge pounced over the surface. This will disperse the paint.

7. Using the mop brush, lightly brush diagonally in the same direction as before across the paint to blend the colours.

8. Using Black paint and the flat brush, paint irregular oval shapes around the Acra Gold.

9. Lightly spatter random areas with a toothbrush dipped in watery Black.

10. Varnish with water-based varnish.

Mother-of-pearl

This luminous finish is very appropriate for small decorative items such as plates and dressing table sets. The background can be either silver gilding or silver paint.

Materials

Materials for gilding, as listed on page 79, including silver leaf (or artist's acrylic Iridescent Silver painted over a base-coat of light grey)

Artists' acrylics:
Pale Blue
Pink
White
Iridescent White (or Interference Blue)

Cotton wadding

Sea sponge

Cotton cloth (or paper towel)

Procedure

1. Prepare and seal the surface.
2. Gild the surface with silver leaf, following the instructions on page 80. (Alternatively, paint with silver over a light grey background.)
3. Mix a watery puddle of each of Pale Blue, Pink and White.
4. Using a ball of cotton wadding, daub the blue colour over about 90% of the surface. Disperse it with a damp cotton cloth dabbed across the surface.
5. When partially dry use a dry cloth to soak up the surplus paint.

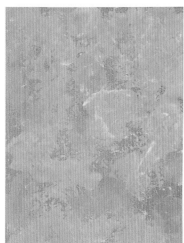

Procedure for mother-of-pearl. Above left, silver-gilded background. Above right, watery blue applied. Below left, watery pink applied. Below right, watery white applied and when dry, Interference Blue added.

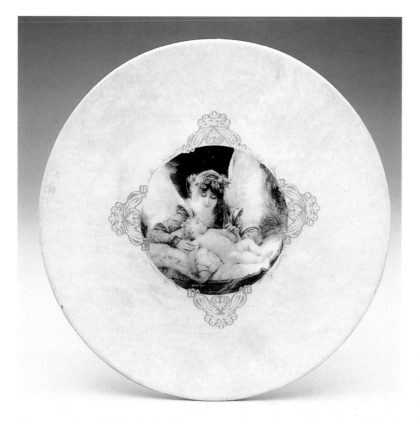

Christening plate with mother-of-pearl finish. Here the final coat of Interference Blue was replaced with Iridescent White.

6. In the same manner, apply pink to about 10% of the surface, allow to partially dry, and soak up excess.

7. Apply white to about 50% of the area, allow to partially dry, and soak up excess. Allow to dry thoroughly.

8. Lightly sponge Iridescent White or Interference Blue over the entire object.

9. When thoroughly dry, apply non-yellowing varnish.

Fresco

Fresco is a technique of wall painting in which pigments mixed in water are applied directly onto freshly laid lime plaster. The colours penetrate the plaster and become part of the wall as it dries.

This effect looks most authentic on larger areas but can be adapted to smaller decorative objects. In adapting fresco for use in découpage, the painted background forms the base onto which is pasted a central image for the fresco—the colours then extended from the picture onto the rest of the surface, using the sponging technique described on page 30. The fresco technique works best using photocopies of extracts from genuine fresco works by the masters of this art form. In

Process for fresco using a detail from a fresco in Villa Lemmi (c. 1483) by Sandro Botticelli.
Colours used here are, clockwise from 10 o'clock:
Base colour—Red Oxide
Glaze 1—White
Glaze 2—Yellow Oxide
Glaze 3—Phthalocyanine Green
Glaze 4—Purple (Maroon + Payne's Grey)
Main colours—White, Purple and Phthalocyanine Green.

choosing colour mixes for the background, select colours from the painted image and its background, especially those colours appearing where the surface of the fresco has cracked to reveal the base. These colours can be used to extend the painting to make the picture and the object appear as one.

Materials

Sealer: either GMV, gesso, Magic Effects Special Paint or interior house paint

Artist's acrylics in colours to match images, plus Burnt Umber for cracks

Scumble medium

No 4 flat brush

No 6 round brush

000 liner brush

GMV

Varnish

Sea sponges, fine and coarse

Cotton cloths

Colour combinations in example

As the choice of colours depend on the colours in the chosen artwork, the colours below are for this particular fresco image. The main colours in this fresco are White, Purple and Green.

Base colour: Red Oxide

Glaze 1: White

Glaze 2: Yellow Oxide

Glaze 3: Phthalocyanine Green

Glaze 4: Purple (1 part Maroon + ½ part Payne's Grey)

(To prepare a glaze, mix 1 part colour to 1 part scumble and 1 part water.)

Procedure

1. Prepare the surface by sanding, sealing and painting on 3 to 5 coats of gesso.

2. Brush on the Red Oxide base colour and allow to dry. Glue down the sealed artwork image.

3. Mix Glaze 1 and brush over surface, right up and onto the edge of the cut fresco image. Dab with a sponge, then rub cotton cloth over glaze in selected areas to allow base colour to show through. Allow to partially dry.

4. Brush on Glaze 2. Dab with a sponge then rub a damp cotton cloth over glaze in uneven patches, allowing some of the base colour and Glaze 1 to show through. Allow to partially dry.

5. Brush on Glaze 3 beside the areas where this colour appears on the fresco. Dab then roll a damp cloth over object, allowing base colour and Glazes 1 and 2 to show through. Allow to partially dry.

6. Brush on Glaze 4 beside the areas where this colour appears on the fresco. Dab then roll a damp cloth over object, allowing the other glazes to show through a little.

7. Identify some cracks or crazes in the fresco picture and, using a liner brush, extend them onto the surface of the object. Dab with the sponge to soften the effect.

8. Apply highlights, using the main colours with a liner brush, and extending a line from clothing or some other element of the picture. Roll the sea sponge lightly across the piece in selected areas, using the main colours and fading to the edges, unites the whole piece with the fresco image.

9. Seal with GMV and apply varnish as required.

HANDY HINTS

- Seal the image before starting the fresco finish to protect the colours.

- Work in small areas at a time.

- Work through the colours, beginning from the base colour, then the background, the main colours and lastly the highlight colours.

Fresco finish on a writing compendium, featuring a portrait of a young girl from a fresco on a wall of ancient Pompeii.

Glossary

Acrylic paint   A synthetic resin-based paint containing pigment.

ASTM   American Society for Testing and Materials. An internationally recognised body which tests paint quality, light fastness, labelling, and includes toxicity standards.

Asymmetrical   Lacking symmetry in design.

Baroque   An art period during the the late 16th to early 18th centuries where audacious architecture and decorative paintings were current.

Black Japan   A black paint based on gilsonite resins and used to stain timber.

Bob   A small cotton-covered sack filled with soft material and used to apply size to objects to eliminate brush marks.

Chamois   Soft, pliable leather or synthetic cloth used to imprint texture on wet paint. Absorption is its chief attribute.

Composition   The arrangement of the parts or elements.

Craquelure   Cracks that develop on the surface of a painting as a result of drying. Mediums can also be applied to achieve the same aged look.

Cross-hatching   Fine lines laid close together and intersecting.

Découpage   The art of designing using cut-out images on surfaces of furniture and decorative objects. Coats of varnish are applied and sanded until the surface is even and as smooth as glass.

Diptych   A picture comprising two panels or leaves. Mostly made on a small scale for portable devotional use.

Distress   To apply mediums to an object to give an aged appearance.

Faux finish   Imitation of something so as to look authentic.

Fresco   An Italian word for 'fresh'. A technique of wall painting in which pigments mixed in water are applied directly to freshly laid plaster.

Gesso A term used to refer to many types of white liquid used to prepare surfaces for painting. It can be made from gypsum, chalk or synthetic adhesives.

Gilding The technique of affixing thin sheets of metal called leaf to a surface. A variety of metals are available, including gold, silver and aluminium.

Gouache An opaque, matte, watercolour paint also known as body colour. Chalk-like filler is added to the pigment to make it opaque. White is added to make brighter tones so light reflects off the paint.

Glaze A transparent layer of paint applied over an opaque layer.

Ground A specially prepared painting surface.

Hatching A technique using closely set parallel lines to indicate tone and suggesting light and shade. Hence cross-hatching.

Hue The common name for a colour.

Icon An image, statue or painting of a sacred personage, itself being regarded as sacred.

Impressionists An innovative group of artists prominent during the 1800s. Their use of colour to show tone and effect without elaborate detail, makes their work easily recognisable.

Incising Using a sharp tool to carve lines into a surface prior to painting.

Intensity The degree of saturation of colour: pale blue is considered less intense than a deep rich blue.

Isocol A product name for a propanol-based alcohol rub. It can be used to react on a painted surface to open the paint to reveal the undercolour.

Lightfast The term applied to pigments that resist fading when exposed to sunlight.

Magic Effects Special Paint A plaster-based paint used to obtain textured and decorative finishes. Very suitable as a filler and available in a variety of colours.

Medium A. The liquid, either oil or acrylic, in which pigments are suspended. B. Chosen material with which the artist works (paint, pencil, pastel, etc.).

Mixed media The use of different media in the same picture.

Monochrome A painting executed in different tints of one colour.

Motif The dominant feature in a composition.

Mural A painting executed directly on or permanently fixed to a wall.

Opaque The covering ability of a pigment to hide an underlying colour.

Palette *A.* A board on which to lay out paint and mix colours. *B.* The colour tonality of a painting.

Patina *A.* The effects of age such as encrustation, yellowing or craquelure on a work. *B.* Commercial product which simulates the effects of aging.

Perspective The technique of representing three-dimensional space on a two-dimensional surface.

Pigment Colouring agents used in paint and drawing media.

Plane The surface onto which a composition is made.

Polytych A picture comprising four or more parts, panels or canvases.

Pouncing Transferring paint onto a pre-painted surface. To pounce, hold a stipple brush perpendicular to the painted surface and with firm pressure apply paint quickly over the area.

Pre-Raphaelite An art period in which a group of artists reverted to a period before the artist Raphael, when subjects were not idealised.

Primary colours Red, yellow and blue.

PVA Polyvinyl acetate, a synthetic resin used as a paint medium and in varnish. A commonly used glue.

Renaissance The revival of art and letters under the influence of classical models in the fourteenth to sixteenth centuries. Style of art and architecture.

Rococo The Rococo style succeeded the Baroque, emerging in Paris in the early eighteenth century. The style dominated in a wide range of arts, including architecture, music and literature, as well as painting. It is distinguished by lightness of decoration and stylistic elegance.

Rottonstone Decomposed siliceous limestone used as polishing powder.

Saturation Intensity or brilliance of a colour

Scumble A. Thin layer of colour placed over a darker underpaint. Scumbles are light and translucent. The presence of the darker underlayer will shift the appearance of the scumble toward a cooler tone. B. Commercially produced medium mixed with paint to retard drying time and retain texture in the paint.

Secondary colours Orange, green, and violet, achieved by mixing the primary colours in various combinations.

Sgraffito An Italian word meaning 'scratched' used to describe a method of making a pattern. Following gilding, the metallic surface was painted over. When dry the painted surface was scratched to reveal the gold beneath. (See Incising.)

Shellac A yellow resin formed from secretions of the lac insect and used in making varnish.

Size A glue solution used to seal an absorbent surface.

Stippling A brushwork technique of making repeated applications of paint with a stiff brush held perpendicular to the surface of the painting.

Symmetrical Balance resulting from the right proportion between the parts of the whole. Similar parts facing each other.

Tint The name of a colour.

Tone The lightness or darkness of a colour corresponding to a grey scale that ranges from white to black.

Translucent The state of allowing light to filter through.

Triptych A picture comprising three panels. In its most common form, the central panel was twice the width of the outer panels or wings, so they could be folded over to close the triptych and protect the images.

Underpainting A preparatory paint layer as a base for a composition and to establish basic areas of light and dark colours.

Value Relative lightness or darkness of a colour, corresponding to a grey scale that ranges from white to black.

Varnish A coating applied to the surface of a painting to protect the paint and bring together the final appearance of the painting. Varnishes are traditionally clear but can be toned or altered with the addition of pigments or mediums. Many varnishes darken with age.

Bibliography and suggested reading

Baker, Joan Stanley 1984, *Japanese Art*, Thames and Hudson Ltd, London.

Beckett, Sister Wendy, 1994, *Sister Wendy's Grand Tour Discovering Europe's Great Art*, BBC Books, London.

Beckett, Sister Wendy & Wright, Patricia 1995, *The Story of Painting: The Essential Guide to the History of Western Art*, Readers Digest Press, Sydney.

Bevlin, Marjorie Elliott 1984, *Design Through Discovery* (4th edition), Holt Rinehart & Winston, New York.

Bindman, Catherine 1993, *Designer's Guide to French Patterns*, Chronicle Books, San Francisco.

Camp, Jeffery 1996, *Paint: A Manual of Pictorial Thought and Practical Advice*, Dorling Kindersley, London.

Carr, Dawson W & Leonard, Mark 1992, *Looking at Paintings: A guide to Technical Terms*, J .Paul Getty Museum, Malibu.

Faulkner, Rupert 1995, *Japanese Studio Crafts: Tradition and the Avant-Garde*, Laurence King, London.

Fowler, H W (ed) 1964, *The Concise Oxford Dictionary of Current English*, OUP, Oxford.

Gage, John 1993, *Colour and Culture: Practice and Meaning from Antiquity to Abstraction*, Thames and Hudson, London.

Gair, Angela 1995, *Collins Artist's Manual: The Complete Guide to Painting and Drawing Materials and Techniques*, Harper Collins Publishers, London.

Gombrick, Ernst H 1995, *The Story of Art* (16th edition), Phaidon, London.

Graves, Maitland 1951, *The Art of Colour and Design* (second edition), McGraw Hill Book Company, The Art School Pratt Institute, New York.

Greenhalgh, Michael & Duro, Paul 1992, *Essential Art History*, Bloomsbury, London.

Guth, Christine 1996, *Japanese Art of the Edo Period*, Calmann and King Ltd, London.

Ingamells, John 1990, *The Wallace Collection*, Scala Publications, London.

Lade, Val 1994, *18th Century Découpage*, Sally Milner Publishing, Sydney.

Marchenko, Elena 1987, *Masters of World Painting in Soviet Museums*, Aurora Art Publishers, Leningrad.

Microsoft Corporation, 1993–1997, *Encarta 98 Encyclopedia*, US.

Piper, Sir David (ed.) 1988, *Dictionary of Art & Artists*, Collins, Glasgow.

de Sausmarez, Maurice 1983, *Basic Design: the dynamics of visual form*, Van Nostrard Reinhold, New York.

Stoops, Jack & Samuelson, Jerry 1983, *Design Dialogue*, Davis Publications, Worcester, Massachusetts.

Swanson, Vern Grosvenor 1997, John William Godward: *The Eclipse of Classicism*, Antique Collectors' Club, Woodbridge, Suffolk.

Thompson, Daniel V 1956, *The Materials and Techniques of Medieval Painting*, Dover Publications Inc, New York.

Suppliers

Australia

New South Wales

Decorating with Découpage
  Penny Haldane
  4 Denise Ave
  Glenbrook NSW 2773
  Phone: (02) 4739 0046
  Fax: (02) 4739 9537
  Webpage: www.decordécoupage.com.au
  (découpage papers — mail order)

Lindfield Decorative Arts Centre
  Angie & Sonny Park
  14 Moore Avenue
  West Lindfield NSW 2070
  Phone: (02) 9416 6428
  Fax: (02) 9416 5408
  (wooden boxes, trays and paper)

Lugarno Craft Cottage
  Frances Robinson
  243 Belmore Road
  Riverwood NSW 2210
  Phone and fax: (02) 9584 1944
  On line shop: www.lugarnocraft.com.au
  (découpage papers and supplies)

South Australia

Jill Higgins
  The Sea House
  2A Chapel Street
  Glenelg SA 5045
  Phone: (08) 8295 7922
  (large range of découpage papers and supplies)

Queensland

Active Abrasives Pty Ltd
Kerry & Ruth Weir
'Delkirk', 10 Seabreeze Road
Manly West Qld 4179
Phone: (07) 3396 4457
Fax: (07) 3396 9330
email: activeabrasives@optusnet.com.au
Web: www.activeabrasives.com
(découpage requirements, Liquitex, sandpaper)

Hobby Craft and Games
Kerry Hagen
Unit 1/4 Belconnen Cr
Brendale Qld 4500
Phone: (07) 3881 2777
Fax: (07) 3889 6232
www.hobbycraftandgames.com
(wooden pieces for découpage, paints and mediums)

Enjoy Paper
Marcia & Richard Stephenson
Tattersalls Arcade, 202 Edward Street
Brisbane Qld 4000
Phone & Fax: (07) 3210 0825

Also: 6 The Brickworks
Warehouse Road
Southport Qld 4215
Ph: (07) 5528 0077
Fax: (07) 5528 0767
(handmade Japanese paper)

Classy Crafts
Shirley Hagen
37 Hall Street
Chermside Qld 4032
Phone: (07) 3359 1922
(découpage papers and supplies)

Victoria

Exquisite Découpage
  Ron & Kerry Kwestroo
  293 Cheltenham Road
  Keysborough Vic 3173
  Phone: (03) 9798 2449
  email: edp1@optushome.com.au

Hof Woodart
  Will Hof
  1060 Doncaster Rd
  Doncaster East Vic 3109
  Phone: (03) 9841 6491
  email: wietsehof@netscape.net
  (woodwork for découpeurs)

Langridge Colours
  David Coles
  120 Langridge Street
  Collingwood Vic 3066
  Phone: (03) 9419 4453
  Fax: (03) 9419 4478
  email: langridg@webtime.com.au
  (crackle varnish, gilding supplies and antiquing mediums)

Romantique
  June Wilhelm
  68 Milton Parade
  Malvern Vic 3144
  Phone: (03) 9822 5293
  Fax: (03) 9804 3665
  Web: www.romantique.com.au
  (papers and supplies)

L'Acqua Terra Ceramics
  Julie Swift
  287 Tindals Road
  Warrandyte Vic 3113
  Phone (mobile): 0419 109686, (03) 9876 5032
  (ceramic supplies)

Tasmania

Crafty Critters
  Suzi Foggo
  15 Abbott Street
  East Launceston 7250
  Phone: 1800 030031
  On line shop: www.craftycritters.com.au

Western Australia

The Craft House
  Ingrid Sims
  210 Nicholson Road
  Subiaco WA 6008
  Phone and fax: 08 9381 2880
  email: isims@iinet.net.au
  (extensive range of papers and requirements)

New Zealand

Dunedin Craft Centre
  90 Crawford Street
  Dunedin
  email: craftcen@es.co.nz
  Phone: 64 3 477 0330
  Fax: 64 3 474 1321

Stitch and Craft
  32 east Tamaki Road
  Hunters Corner
  Papatoetoe, Auckland
  email: pauline@stitchandcraft.co.nz
  Phone: (09) 278 1351
  Fax: (09) 278 1356

United States

Aiko's Art Materials
  Chuck Izui
  3347 N. Clark Street
  Chicago, Il 60657 USA
  Phone: 773 404-5600
  Fax: 773 404-5919
  email: aikosart@aol.com
  (handmade Japanese papers)

Ichiyo Art Center
  Hiroshi & Elaine Jo
  432 East Paces Ferry Road
  Atlanta, GA 30305 USA
  Phone: 404-233-1846
  Fax: 404-233-8012
  email: ichiyoart@aol.com
  (Japanese paper)

United Kingdom

Museums and Galleries Marketing Ltd
  Unit 12, Manor Furlong
  Marston Trading Estate
  Frome, Somerset B A114RL, UK
  Phone: (44) 1373 462165
  Fax: (44) 1373 462367
  (papers)

The Medici Society
  Grafton House, Hyde Estate Road
  London, NW9 6JZ, UK
  Phone: 020 8205 2500
  Fax: 020 8205 2552
  Web: www.medici.co.uk
  (fine art greeting cards, prints)

The Fitzwilliam Museum
  University of Cambridge
  Trumpington Street
  Cambridge CB21RB UK
  Phone: (44) 1223 332914
  (papers)

Ornamenta.Co. UK
  3/12 Chelsea Harbour Design Centre
  London SW10 0XE UK
  Phone: (44) 171 352 1824
  Fax: (44) 171 376 3398
  http://www.ornamenta.co.uk
  (prints)

Découpage Guilds

Membership in a découpage guild provides a support network which both helps members achieve quality work and keeps them up to date with latest techniques and products. Friendships made from within the guild can become a very valuable offshoot to this art form and I'm sure life is enriched for many people as a result, and the world a better place because of it. Enjoyment from creating découpage is a certainty.

Découpage Guild Australia Inc.
  Glenda Swift
  Phone: (03) 9878 1080

Découpage Guild NSW Inc.
  Mary Waks
  Phone: (02) 9665 4670

Découpage Guild Queensland Inc.
  Myra Givans
  Phone/Fax: (07) 3862 9868

National Guild of Découpeurs (USA)
  Margo Tuell
  Phone: 8022533903
  email: MDPeer@aol.com
  www.découpage.org

Guild of British Découpeurs
  Roy Larking
  Fax: 44 181 660 7725
  email: kbk58@dial.pipex.com.uk